BREAD

Breads, rolls, coffee cakes, quick breads,
biscuits, muffins, scones and more

Publications International, Ltd.

Photography on pages 47, 63, 69, 71, 73 and 77 by PIL Photo Studio North.

Pictured on the front cover *(top to bottom):* Brown Soda Bread *(page 118)* and Cinnamon Raisin Bread
(page 26).

Pictured on the back cover *(left to right):* Lemon-Glazed Zucchini Muffins *(page 168),* Sandwich Bread
(page 4) and Tomato and Cheese Focaccia *(page 82).*

ISBN: 978-1-4508-8795-3

Library of Congress Control Number: 2014934000

Manufactured in China.

8 7 6 5 4 3 2 1

Microwave Cooking: Microwave ovens vary in wattage. Use the cooking times as guidelines and check
for doneness before adding more time.

Publications International, Ltd.

CONTENTS

CLASSIC YEAST BREADS

SANDWICH BREAD

½ cup milk

3 tablespoons butter

3 tablespoons sugar

2 teaspoons salt

2 packages (¼ ounce each)
   active dry yeast

1½ cups warm water
   (105° to 115°F)

5 to 6 cups all-purpose flour,
   divided

Makes 2 loaves

1. Combine milk, butter, sugar and salt in small saucepan; heat over low heat until butter melts and sugar dissolves. Cool to 105°F.

2. Dissolve yeast in warm water in large bowl of stand mixer. Add milk mixture and 3 cups flour; beat at low speed with paddle attachment 2 minutes. Add remaining flour, ½ cup at a time; beat until soft dough forms.

3. Replace paddle attachment with dough hook; knead at low speed about 5 minutes or until dough is smooth and elastic. Dough will be slightly sticky to the touch.

4. Shape dough into a ball. Place dough in greased bowl; turn to grease top. Cover and let rise in warm place about 1 hour or until doubled in size.

5. Spray two 8×4-inch loaf pans with nonstick cooking spray. Punch down dough. Divide dough in half; shape each half into loaf. Place in prepared pans; cover and let rise in warm place about 1 hour or until doubled in size. Preheat oven to 400°F.

6. Bake loaves 30 minutes or until golden brown. Remove to wire racks to cool completely.

OATMEAL RAISIN NUT BREAD

2 to 2½ cups bread flour, divided

1 cup old-fashioned oats

1 package (¼ ounce) rapid-rise active dry yeast

1½ teaspoons salt

1½ teaspoons ground cinnamon

1 cup plus 2 tablespoons warm water (120°F)

¼ cup maple syrup

2 tablespoons canola oil

1 cup raisins

¾ cup chopped pecans

Makes 1 loaf

1. Whisk 1 cup flour, oats, yeast, salt and cinnamon in large bowl of stand mixer. Combine warm water, maple syrup and oil in medium bowl. Add to flour mixture; beat at medium speed with paddle attachment 3 minutes.

2. Replace paddle attachment with dough hook. Add enough remaining flour, ½ cup at a time, to make soft dough. Knead at low speed 6 to 8 minutes or until dough is smooth and elastic. Add raisins and pecans; knead until well incorporated.

3. Shape dough into a ball. Place dough in greased bowl; turn to grease top. Cover and let rise in warm place about 40 minutes or until doubled in size.

4. Spray 9×5-inch loaf pan with nonstick cooking spray. Punch down dough. Roll out dough into 14×8-inch rectangle on lightly floured surface. Starting with short side, roll up tightly jelly-roll style; pinch seam to seal. Place seam side down in prepared loaf pan. Cover and let rise about 30 minutes or until doubled in size. Preheat oven to 375°F.

5. Bake 30 to 35 minutes or until golden brown and loaf sounds hollow when tapped. Remove to wire rack to cool completely.

CLASSIC DELI PUMPERNICKEL BREAD

1 cup cold strong coffee*

½ cup finely chopped onion

½ cup molasses

2 tablespoons butter

1 tablespoon salt

2 packages (¼ ounce each) active dry yeast

½ cup warm water (105° to 115°F)

2½ cups bread flour, divided

1 cup whole wheat flour

¼ cup unsweetened cocoa powder

1 tablespoon caraway seeds

2 cups medium rye flour

Cornmeal

Melted butter (optional)

Use fresh brewed coffee or instant coffee granules prepared according to package directions.

Makes 2 loaves

1. Combine coffee, onion, molasses, 2 tablespoons butter and salt in medium saucepan; heat over medium heat to 115° to 120°F.

2. Meanwhile, dissolve yeast in warm water in large bowl of stand mixer; let stand 5 minutes. Stir in coffee mixture. Add 2 cups bread flour, whole wheat flour, cocoa and caraway seeds; beat at low speed with paddle attachment 2 minutes. Add rye flour, ½ cup at a time; beat until dough begins to form a ball.

3. Replace paddle attachment with dough hook. Add enough remaining bread flour, 1 tablespoon at a time, if necessary to prevent sticking. Knead at low speed 5 to 7 minutes or until dough is smooth and elastic.

4. Shape dough into a ball. Place dough in greased bowl; turn to grease top. Cover and let rise in warm place 2 hours or until doubled in size.

5. Line two baking sheets with parchment paper; sprinkle with cornmeal. Punch down dough. Divide dough in half; shape each half into a round, slightly flattened loaf. Place on prepared baking sheets. Cover and let rise in warm place 1 hour or until almost doubled in size. Preheat oven to 375°F.

6. Bake 30 to 35 minutes or until loaves sound hollow when tapped. Remove to wire racks to cool completely. Brush tops of loaves with melted butter, if desired.

SOFT PRETZELS

1 **package (¼ ounce) active dry yeast**

¼ **cup warm water (105° to 115°F)**

3¾ **to 4 cups all-purpose flour, divided**

1 **cup brown ale, at room temperature**

1 **tablespoon sugar**

1 **tablespoon olive oil**

1 **teaspoon coarse salt, divided**

2 **cups hot water**

1 **teaspoon baking soda**

1 **egg, well beaten**

2 **tablespoons butter, melted**

Mustard (optional)

Makes 12 pretzels

1. Dissolve yeast in warm water in large bowl of stand mixer; let stand 5 minutes or until bubbly. Add 2 cups flour, ale, sugar, oil and ¾ teaspoon salt; beat at medium speed with paddle attachment 2 minutes. Add 1¾ cups flour; beat at low speed until soft dough forms.

2. Replace paddle attachment with dough hook. Add enough remaining flour, 1 tablespoon at a time, if necessary to prevent sticking. Knead at low speed 5 to 7 minutes or until dough is smooth and elastic.

3. Shape dough into a ball. Place dough in greased bowl; turn to grease top. Cover and let rise in warm place 45 minutes or until doubled in size.

4. Punch down dough. Divide dough into 12 pieces; roll each piece into rope about 20 inches long. If dough becomes too difficult to roll, let stand 10 minutes. Shape ropes into pretzels.

5. Line baking sheets with parchment paper. Preheat oven to 425°F. Combine hot water and baking soda in shallow dish. Dip pretzels into baking soda mixture; place on prepared baking sheets. Cover loosely and let rise in warm place 15 to 20 minutes. Brush pretzels with egg; sprinkle with remaining ¼ teaspoon salt.

6. Bake 10 minutes or until golden brown. Brush pretzels with melted butter. Serve with mustard, if desired.

Variation: Sprinkle a small amount of grated cheese over the pretzels before baking—Parmesan, Asiago or Cheddar are good choices. Or add ½ cup (2 ounces) Cheddar cheese to the dough with the flour in step 2.

THREE-GRAIN BREAD

1 cup milk

2 tablespoons honey

3 teaspoons olive oil

1 teaspoon salt

1 cup whole wheat flour

¾ cup all-purpose flour

1 package (¼ ounce) rapid-rise active dry yeast

½ cup plus 1 tablespoon old-fashioned oats, divided

¼ cup whole grain cornmeal, plus additional for baking sheet

1 egg beaten with 1 tablespoon water

Makes 1 loaf

1. Combine milk, honey, oil and salt in small saucepan; heat over low heat to 115° to 120°F.

2. Whisk whole wheat flour, all-purpose flour and yeast in large bowl of stand mixer. Add milk mixture; beat at medium speed with paddle attachment 3 minutes. Beat in ½ cup oats and ¼ cup cornmeal at low speed. If dough is too wet, add additional flour, 1 teaspoon at a time, until dough begins to come together.

3. Replace paddle attachment with dough hook; knead at low speed 5 minutes or until dough is smooth and elastic.

4. Shape dough into a ball. Place dough in greased bowl; turn to grease top. Cover and let rise in warm place about 1 hour or until dough is puffy and does not spring back when touched.

5. Sprinkle baking sheet lightly with cornmeal. Punch down dough; shape into 8-inch loaf. Place on prepared baking sheet. Cover and let rise in warm place about 45 minutes or until almost doubled in size. Preheat oven to 375°F.

6. Cut shallow slash down center of loaf with sharp knife. Brush lightly with egg mixture; sprinkle with remaining 1 tablespoon oats.

7. Bake 30 minutes or until loaf sounds hollow when tapped and internal temperature reaches 200°F. Remove to wire rack to cool completely.

HERBED POTATO ROLLS

2½ cups bread flour, divided

½ cup instant potato flakes

1 tablespoon sugar

1 package (¼ ounce) rapid-rise active dry yeast

1¼ teaspoons dried rosemary

1 teaspoon salt

¼ teaspoon black pepper

1 cup warm milk (120°F)

1½ tablespoons olive oil

1 egg, beaten

Poppy seeds, sesame seeds and/or additional dried rosemary (optional)

Makes 12 rolls

1. Whisk 1 cup flour, potato flakes, sugar, yeast, rosemary, salt and pepper in large bowl of stand mixer. Add warm milk and oil; beat at medium speed with paddle attachment 2 minutes.

2. Replace paddle attachment with dough hook. Add enough remaining flour, ½ cup at a time, to make soft dough. Knead at medium-low speed 6 to 8 minutes or until dough is smooth and elastic.

3. Shape dough into a ball. Place dough in greased bowl; turn to grease top. Cover and let rise in warm place about 1 hour or until doubled in size.

4. Line large baking sheet with parchment paper. Punch down dough. Divide dough into 12 pieces; roll each piece into 10-inch rope on lightly floured surface. Shape each rope into a coil, tucking end under coil. Place 2 inches apart on prepared baking sheet. Cover and let rise in warm place about 40 minutes or until doubled in size.

5. Preheat oven to 375°F Brush rolls with egg; sprinkle with toppings, if desired.

6. Bake 20 to 25 minutes or until golden brown. Remove to wire rack to cool. Serve warm or at room temperature.

GANNAT (FRENCH CHEESE BREAD)

1 package (¼ ounce) active
   dry yeast

1 teaspoon sugar

4 to 6 tablespoons warm water
   (105° to 115°F), divided

2½ cups all-purpose flour

¼ cup (½ stick) butter,
   softened

1 teaspoon salt

2 eggs

1 cup (4 ounces) shredded
   Emmentaler, Gruyère or
   sharp Cheddar cheese,

1 teaspoon vegetable oil

Makes 1 loaf

1. Dissolve yeast and sugar in 4 tablespoons water in small bowl; let stand 5 minutes or until bubbly.

2. Combine flour, butter and salt in food processor; process 15 seconds or until blended. Add yeast mixture and eggs; process 15 seconds or until blended.

3. With motor running, slowly drizzle just enough water through feed tube so dough forms a ball that cleans side of bowl. Process until ball turns around bowl about 25 times. Let dough rest 1 to 2 minutes.

4. With motor running, slowly drizzle in enough remaining water to make dough soft, smooth and satiny but not sticky. Process until dough turns around bowl about 15 times.

5. Turn dough out onto lightly floured surface; shape into a ball. Place dough in greased bowl; turn to grease top. Cover and let rise in warm place about 1 hour or until doubled in size.

6. Spray 9-inch round cake or pie pan with nonstick cooking spray. Punch down dough. Place dough on lightly greased surface; knead cheese into dough. Roll or pat into 8-inch circle. Place dough in prepared pan; brush with oil. Cover and let rise in warm place about 45 minutes or until doubled in size. Preheat oven to 375°F.

7. Bake 30 to 35 minutes or until golden brown and loaf sounds hollow when tapped. Remove to wire rack to cool completely.

BREAD BOWLS

3 to 3½ cups bread flour, divided

¼ cup white cornmeal, plus additional for baking sheet

1 package (¼ ounce) rapid-rise active dry yeast

2 teaspoons sugar

1½ teaspoons salt

1⅓ cups warm water (120°F)

Makes 4 bread bowls

1. Whisk 1 cup flour, ¼ cup cornmeal, yeast, sugar and salt in large bowl of stand mixer. Add warm water; beat at medium speed with paddle attachment 2 minutes.

2. Replace paddle attachment with dough hook. Add enough remaining flour, ½ cup at a time, to make firm dough. Knead at low speed 5 minutes or until dough is smooth and elastic.

3. Shape dough into a ball. Place dough in greased bowl; turn to grease top. Cover loosely and let rise in warm place about 30 minutes or until doubled in size.

4. Line large baking sheet with parchment paper; sprinkle with cornmeal. Turn out dough onto lightly floured surface; punch down dough. Divide dough into four pieces; shape into round balls. Place on prepared baking sheet. Cover loosely and let rise in warm place about 30 minutes or doubled in size. Preheat oven to 425°F.

5. Bake 20 to 25 minutes or until loaves sound hollow when tapped. For a crisper crust, spray loaves with cold water several times during first 10 minutes of baking. Remove to wire rack to cool completely.

6. To make bread bowls, cut thin slice from top of each loaf. Remove inside of bread, leaving ½-inch shell on bottom and sides of loaves. (Reserve inside bread for bread crumbs or another use.) If desired, bake bowls in 300°F oven 10 minutes to dry out bread slightly.

NEW YORK RYE BREAD

2 cups warm water
(105° to 115°F)

⅓ cup packed brown sugar

2 tablespoons vegetable oil

1 tablespoon salt

1 package (¼ ounce) active
dry yeast

2 to 2½ cups bread flour,
divided

1 tablespoon caraway seeds

2 cups rye flour

1 cup whole wheat flour

Cornmeal

Makes 2 loaves

1. Combine warm water, brown sugar, oil, salt, and yeast in large bowl of stand mixer; stir until yeast is dissolved.

2. Add 2 cups bread flour and caraway seeds; beat at low speed with paddle attachment 2 minutes. Add rye flour and wheat flour, ½ cup at a time; beat until dough begins to form a ball.

3. Replace paddle attachment with dough hook. Add enough remaining bread flour, 1 tablespoon at a time, if necessary to prevent sticking. Knead at low speed 5 to 7 minutes or until dough is smooth and elastic.

4. Shape dough into a ball. Place dough in greased bowl; turn to grease top. Cover and let rise in warm place 1½ to 2 hours or until doubled in size.

5. Line large baking sheet with parchment paper; sprinkle with cornmeal. Punch down dough. Divide dough in half; shape each half into 10-inch oblong-shaped loaf. Place on prepared baking sheet. Cover and let rise in warm place 45 minutes to 1 hour or until almost doubled in size. Preheat oven to 375°F.

6. Spray or brush loaves with cool water. Cut three ¼-inch-deep slashes on top of each loaf with serrated knife.

7. Bake 25 to 30 minutes or until loaves sound hollow when tapped. Remove to wire racks to cool completely.

DINNER ROLLS

1¼ **cups milk**

½ **cup shortening**

3¾ **to 4¼ cups all-purpose flour, divided**

¼ **cup sugar**

2 **packages (¼ ounce each) active dry yeast**

1 **teaspoon salt**

2 **eggs**

Makes 24 rolls

1. Combine milk and shortening in small saucepan; heat over low heat to 110° to 120°F. (Shortening does not need to melt completely.)

2. Whisk 1½ cups flour, sugar, yeast and salt in large bowl of stand mixer. Gradually add milk mixture; beat at low speed with paddle attachment until well blended. Add eggs and 1 cup flour; beat at medium speed 2 minutes. Beat in enough additional flour, about 1¼ cups, to make soft dough.

3. Replace paddle attachment with dough hook. Add enough remaining flour, 1 tablespoon at a time, if necessary to prevent sticking; knead at low speed 5 to 7 minutes or until dough is smooth and elastic.

4. Shape dough into a ball. Place dough in greased bowl; turn to grease top. Cover and let rise in warm place 1 hour or until doubled in size.

5. Punch down dough; knead on lightly floured surface 1 minute. Cover with towel; let rest 10 minutes. Spray two 8-inch square baking pans with nonstick cooking spray. Divide dough in half. Cut one half into 12 pieces, keeping remaining half covered with towel. Shape pieces into balls; place in rows in one prepared pan. Repeat with remaining dough. Cover and let rise in warm place 30 minutes or until doubled in size. Preheat oven to 375°F.

6. Bake 15 to 20 minutes or until golden brown. Remove to wire racks to cool slightly. Serve warm.

FARMER-STYLE SOUR CREAM BREAD

1 cup sour cream, at room
   temperature

3 tablespoons water

2½ to 3 cups all-purpose flour,
   divided

2 tablespoons sugar

1 package (¼ ounce) active
   dry yeast

1½ teaspoons salt

¼ teaspoon baking soda

Vegetable oil

1 tablespoon sesame or
   poppy seeds

Makes 1 loaf

1. Combine sour cream and water in small saucepan; heat over low heat to 110° to 120°F.

2. Whisk 2 cups flour, sugar, yeast, salt and baking soda in large bowl of stand mixer. Add sour cream mixture; beat at low speed with paddle attachment 3 minutes.

3. Replace paddle attachment with dough hook. Add remaining flour, ¼ cup at a time; knead at low speed 5 to 7 minutes or until dough is smooth and elastic.

4. Line large baking sheet with parchment paper. Shape dough into a ball; place on prepared baking sheet. Flatten into 8-inch circle. Brush top of loaf with oil; sprinkle with sesame seeds. Invert large bowl over dough and let rise in warm place 1 hour or until doubled in size. Preheat oven to 350°F.

5. Bake 22 to 27 minutes or until golden brown. Remove to wire rack to cool completely.

CINNAMON RAISIN BREAD

1 **cup milk**

3 **tablespoons butter**

3 **to 3½ cups all-purpose flour, divided**

½ **cup sugar, divided**

1 **package (¼ ounce) rapid-rise active dry yeast**

1 **teaspoon salt**

1 **whole egg**

1 **egg, separated**

1 **teaspoon vanilla**

¾ **cup raisins**

1 **tablespoon ground cinnamon**

1 **tablespoon butter, melted**

1 **cup raisins**

1 **tablespoon water**

Makes 1 loaf

1. Combine milk and 3 tablespoons butter in small saucepan; heat over low heat to 115° to 120°F (butter does not need to melt completely).

2. Whisk 1½ cups flour, ¼ cup sugar, yeast and salt in large bowl of stand mixer. Gradually add milk mixture; beat at low speed with paddle attachment until blended. Beat at medium speed 2 minutes. Add whole egg, egg yolk and vanilla; beat 2 minutes. Beat in enough additional flour, about 1½ cups, to make soft dough.

3. Replace paddle attachment with dough hook. Knead at low speed about 5 minutes or until dough is smooth and elastic. Add enough remaining flour, 1 tablespoon at a time, if necessary to clean side of bowl. Add raisins; knead at low speed until incorporated. (Dough will be soft and sticky.) Knead several times; shape dough into a ball. Place dough in greased bowl; turn to grease top. Cover and let rise in warm place about 1 hour or until doubled in size.

4. Punch down dough; knead on lightly floured surface 1 minute. Cover and let rest 10 minutes. Spray 9×5-inch loaf pan with nonstick cooking spray. Combine remaining ¼ cup sugar and cinnamon in small bowl; reserve 1 teaspoon mixture for top of loaf, if desired.

5. Roll dough into 20×9-inch rectangle with lightly floured rolling pin. Brush with 1 tablespoon melted butter; sprinkle with cinnamon-sugar. Starting with short side, roll up dough jelly-roll style. Pinch ends and seam to seal. Place loaf, seam side down, in prepared pan; cover and let rise in warm place about 30 minutes or until doubled in size.

6. Preheat oven to 375°F. Beat egg white and water in small bowl. Brush over top of loaf; sprinkle with reserved cinnamon-sugar, if desired.

7. Bake 40 to 45 minutes or until loaf sounds hollow when tapped and internal temperature reaches 190°F. Cover loosely with foil halfway through baking time if loaf is browning too fast. Immediately remove from pan; cool completely on wire rack.

WHOLE WHEAT HERB BREAD

⅔ cup water

⅔ cup milk

2 teaspoons sugar

2 packages (¼ ounce each) active dry yeast

3 egg whites, lightly beaten

3 tablespoons olive oil

1 teaspoon salt

½ teaspoon dried basil

½ teaspoon dried oregano

4 to 4½ cups whole wheat flour, divided

Makes 4 small loaves

1. Bring water to a boil in small saucepan over medium heat. Remove from heat; stir in milk and sugar. When mixture cools to 110° to 115°F, stir in yeast; let stand 10 minutes or until bubbly.

2. Combine egg whites, oil, salt, basil and oregano in large bowl of stand mixer; beat at medium speed with paddle attachment until blended. Add yeast mixture; mix well. Add 1½ cups flour; beat 2 minutes. Add 2½ cups flour, ½ cup at a time; beat until dough forms a rough ball.

3. Replace paddle attachment with dough hook. Add enough remaining flour, 1 tablespoon at a time, if necessary to clean side of bowl. Knead at low speed 5 to 7 minutes or until dough is smooth and elastic.

4. Shape dough into a ball. Place dough in greased bowl; turn to grease top. Cover and let rise in warm place about 1 hour or until doubled in size.

5. Preheat oven to 350°F. Line large baking sheet with parchment paper. Punch down dough; place on lightly floured surface. Divide dough into four pieces; roll each piece into a ball. Place on prepared baking sheet.

6. Bake 30 to 35 minutes or until golden brown and loaves sound hollow when tapped. Remove to wire rack to cool completely.

EGG BAGELS

1 package (¼ ounce) active dry yeast

2 tablespoons plus 1 teaspoon sugar, divided

½ to ¾ cup warm water (105° to 115°F), divided

2½ cups all-purpose flour

1 tablespoon canola oil

1 teaspoon salt

2 eggs, divided

2 quarts water

2 tablespoons sugar

2 tablespoons cold water

Makes 12 bagels

1. Dissolve yeast and 1 teaspoon sugar in ¼ cup warm water in small bowl; let stand 5 minutes or until bubbly.

2. Combine flour, oil and salt in food processor; process 5 seconds or just until blended. Add yeast mixture and 1 egg; process 10 seconds or until blended. With motor running, slowly drizzle just enough warm water through feed tube until dough forms a ball. Process until ball turns around bowl about 25 times. Let dough rest 1 to 2 minutes.

3. With motor running, slowly drizzle in enough remaining warm water to make dough soft, smooth and satiny but not sticky. Process until dough turns around bowl about 15 times. Shape dough into a ball. Place dough in greased bowl; turn to grease top. Cover and let rise 15 minutes.

4. Line baking sheets with parchment paper. Divide dough into 12 pieces; roll each piece into 6-inch rope. Bring ends of each piece together to form circle; moisten ends and pinch together to seal. Place on prepared baking sheets; let rest 15 minutes.

5. Combine 2 quarts water and remaining 2 tablespoons sugar in large saucepan or Dutch oven; bring to a boil over medium-high heat. Working in batches, gently place bagels in boiling water. When they rise to the surface, turn and cook 2 minutes or until puffy. Use slotted spoon to remove bagels from water; return to baking sheets.

6. Preheat oven to 425°F. Beat remaining egg and 2 tablespoons cold water in small bowl; brush over bagels.

7. Bake 20 to 25 minutes or until crusts are golden and crisp. Remove to wire racks to cool.

RUSTIC FAVORITES

WALNUT FIG BREAD

1 cup honey beer

2 tablespoons butter

1 tablespoon honey

2¼ cups all-purpose flour, divided

1 cup whole wheat flour

1 tablespoon fennel seeds

1 package (¼ ounce) active dry yeast

1½ teaspoons salt

1 egg, beaten

1 cup chopped dried figs

½ cup chopped walnuts, toasted

Makes 1 loaf

1. Combine beer, butter and honey in small saucepan; heat over low heat to 120°F.

2. Whisk 1 cup all-purpose flour, whole wheat flour, fennel seeds, yeast and salt in large bowl of stand mixer. Add beer mixture; beat at medium-low speed with paddle attachment 3 minutes. Add egg; beat until blended. Add remaining all-purpose flour, ¼ cup at a time, to make soft dough. Beat in figs and walnuts.

3. Replace paddle attachment with dough hook; knead at low speed about 5 minutes or until dough is smooth and elastic.

4. Shape dough into a ball. Place dough in greased bowl; turn to grease top. Cover and let rise in warm place about 1 hour or until doubled in size.

5. Line baking sheet with parchment paper. Punch down dough. Shape dough into round loaf; place on prepared baking sheet. Cover and let rise in warm place 40 minutes or until doubled in size. Preheat oven to 350°F.

6. Bake 30 to 35 minutes or until golden brown and loaf sounds hollow when tapped. Remove to wire rack to cool completely.

SOUR CREAM AND ONION ROLLS

1 **tablespoon butter**

1 **cup chopped onion**

3¼ **cups all-purpose flour, divided**

1 **tablespoon sugar**

1 **package (¼ ounce) rapid-rise active dry yeast**

1 **teaspoon salt**

1 **cup warm beer (120°F)**

½ **cup sour cream**

2 **tablespoons butter, melted**

Makes 12 rolls

1. Spray 10-inch pie plate with nonstick cooking spray. Melt 1 tablespoon butter in small skillet over medium-high heat. Add onion; cook and stir 3 to 4 minutes or until tender.

2. Whisk 2 cups flour, sugar, yeast and salt in large bowl of stand mixer. Add warm beer; beat at low speed with paddle attachment until blended. Add sour cream; beat at medium-high speed 2 minutes.

3. Replace paddle attachment with dough hook. Add ½ cup onion; knead until incorporated. Add enough remaining flour, ¼ cup at a time, to make soft dough. Knead at low speed 3 minutes or until dough is smooth and elastic.

4. Shape dough into 12 balls with greased hands. Smooth tops of balls; place in prepared pie plate. Cover loosely and let rise in warm place 20 minutes.

5. Preheat oven to 400°F. Brush tops of rolls with melted butter; sprinkle with remaining onion.

6. Bake 25 to 30 minutes or until lightly browned. Cool slightly in pan on wire rack. Serve warm or at room temperature.

SUGAR AND SPICE BREAD

1 **cup milk**

¼ **cup (½ stick) butter**

2 **cups bread flour, divided**

¼ **cup packed brown sugar**

1 **package (¼ ounce) rapid-rise active dry yeast**

2 **teaspoons ground cinnamon**

1 **teaspoon salt**

¼ **teaspoon ground nutmeg**

⅛ **teaspoon ground cloves**

Makes 1 loaf

1. Combine milk and butter in small saucepan; heat over medium heat to 120°F (butter does not need to melt completely).

2. Whisk 1 cup flour, brown sugar, yeast, cinnamon, salt, nutmeg and cloves in large bowl of stand mixer. Add milk mixture; beat at medium speed with paddle attachment 2 minutes.

3. Replace paddle attachment with dough hook. Add enough remaining flour, ¼ cup at a time, to make soft dough. Knead at medium-low speed 5 to 7 minutes or until dough is smooth and elastic.

4. Shape dough into a ball. Place dough in greased bowl; turn to grease top. Cover and let rise in warm place 45 minutes or until doubled in size.

5. Spray 9×5-inch loaf pan with nonstick cooking spray. Punch down dough. Shape dough into loaf; place in prepared pan. Cover loosely and let rise in warm place 30 minutes or until doubled in size. Preheat oven to 375°F.

6. Bake about 30 minutes or until browned and loaf sounds hollow when tapped. Remove to wire rack to cool completely.

PEPPERONI CHEESE BREAD

1 **cup warm beer
(110° to 115°F)**

½ **cup warm milk
(110° to 115°F)**

1 **package (¼ ounce)
active dry yeast**

2¼ **cups all-purpose flour,
divided**

1 **cup rye flour**

1 **tablespoon dried basil**

1 **teaspoon sugar**

1 **teaspoon salt**

1 **teaspoon red pepper flakes**

1 **cup (4 ounces) shredded
sharp Cheddar cheese**

1 **cup finely chopped
pepperoni**

1 **tablespoon olive oil
(optional)**

Makes 2 loaves

1. Combine warm beer and milk in large bowl of stand mixer. Stir in yeast; let stand 5 minutes. Add 2 cups all-purpose flour, rye flour, basil, sugar, salt and red pepper flakes; beat at low speed with paddle attachment 2 minutes.

2. Replace paddle attachment with dough hook. Add enough remaining all-purpose flour, 1 tablespoon at a time, to make stiff dough. Add cheese and pepperoni; knead until incorporated. Knead at low speed 5 minutes or until dough is smooth and elastic.

3. Shape dough into a ball. Place dough in greased bowl; turn to grease top. Cover and let rise in warm place about 1 hour or until doubled in size.

4. Line baking sheets with parchment paper. Punch down dough. Divide dough in half; shape each half into 12-inch loaf. Place on prepared baking sheets. Cover and let rise in warm place about 45 minutes or until doubled in size. Preheat oven to 350°F.

5. Bake 30 to 35 minutes or until golden brown. Brush tops of loaves with oil, if desired. Remove to wire racks to cool completely.

Tip: Serve bread with an oregano-infused dipping oil. Combine 2 tablespoons olive oil, 1 tablespoon chopped green olives, ½ teaspoon black pepper and 1 sprig fresh oregano. Let stand several hours to blend flavors.

ROASTED RED PEPPER BREAD

2 to 2½ cups all-purpose flour, divided

1 cup whole wheat flour

2 tablespoons grated Parmesan cheese

1 package (¼ ounce) rapid-rise active dry yeast

1 teaspoon dried rosemary

½ teaspoon salt

¼ teaspoon dried thyme

1¼ cups warm water (120° to 130°F)

1 tablespoon olive or vegetable oil

½ cup chopped roasted red pepper

1 egg white

2 teaspoons water

Additional dried rosemary (optional)

Makes 1 large loaf or 2 small loaves

1. Whisk 1 cup all-purpose flour, whole wheat flour, Parmesan, yeast, 1 teaspoon rosemary, salt and thyme in large bowl of stand mixer. Add warm water and oil; beat with paddle attachment at low speed until smooth. Beat in roasted pepper.

2. Replace paddle attachment with dough hook. Add enough remaining all-purpose flour, ½ cup at a time, to make soft dough. Knead at low speed about 3 minutes or until dough is smooth and elastic.

3. Shape dough into a ball. Place dough in greased bowl; turn to grease top. Cover and let rise in warm place 30 minutes or until doubled in size.

4. Line baking sheet with parchment paper. Punch down dough. Shape dough into one large or two small round loaves; place on prepared baking sheet. Cover and let rise 30 minutes or until doubled in size.

5. Preheat oven to 375°F. Slash top of loaf with sharp knife. Beat egg white and 2 teaspoons water in small bowl. Brush over top of loaf; sprinkle with additional rosemary, if desired.

6. Bake 35 to 40 minutes for large loaf (25 to 30 minutes for small loaves) or until golden brown and loaf sounds hollow when tapped. Remove to wire rack to cool completely.

PROSCIUTTO PROVOLONE ROLLS

3 cups all-purpose flour, divided

1 package (¼ ounce) rapid-rise active dry yeast

1¼ teaspoons salt

1 cup warm water (120°F)

2 tablespoons olive oil

⅓ cup garlic and herb spreadable cheese

6 thin slices prosciutto (3-ounce package)

6 slices (1 ounce each) provolone cheese

Makes 12 rolls

1. Whisk 1½ cups flour, yeast and salt in large bowl of stand mixer. Add water and oil; beat at medium speed with paddle attachment 2 minutes.

2. Replace paddle attachment with dough hook. Add remaining 1½ cups flour; knead at medium speed about 2 minutes to make soft dough that cleans side of bowl. Knead at medium-low speed 6 to 8 minutes or until dough is smooth and elastic.

3. Shape dough into a ball. Place dough in greased bowl; turn to grease top. Cover and let rise in warm place about 30 minutes or until doubled in size.

4. Spray 12 standard (2½-inch) muffin cups with nonstick cooking spray. Punch down dough. Roll out dough into 12×10-inch rectangle on lightly floured surface.

5. Spread garlic and herb cheese evenly over dough. Arrange prosciutto slices over herb cheese; top with provolone slices. Starting with long side, roll up dough jelly-roll style; pinch seam to seal. Cut crosswise into 1-inch slices; arrange slices, cut sides up, in prepared muffin cups. Cover and let rise in warm place about 25 minutes or until almost doubled in size. Preheat oven to 375°F.

6. Bake about 20 minutes or until golden brown. Loosen edges of rolls with knife; remove to wire rack. Serve warm.

CRUNCHY WHOLE GRAIN BREAD

2 cups warm water (105° to 115°F), divided

⅓ cup honey

2 tablespoons vegetable oil

1 tablespoon salt

2 packages (¼ ounce each) active dry yeast

2 to 2½ cups whole wheat flour, divided

1 cup bread flour

1¼ cups quick oats, divided

½ cup hulled pumpkin seeds or sunflower kernels

½ cup assorted grains and seeds

1 egg white

1 tablespoon water

Makes 2 loaves

1. Combine 1½ cups water, honey, oil and salt in small saucepan; heat over low heat to 115°F to 120°F, stirring occasionally.

2. Dissolve yeast in remaining ½ cup warm water in large bowl of stand mixer; let stand 5 minutes. Stir in honey mixture. Add 1 cup whole wheat flour and bread flour; beat at low speed with paddle attachment 2 minutes.

3. Replace paddle attachment with dough hook. Gradually add 1 cup oats, pumpkin seeds and assorted grains; knead at low speed until incorporated. Add remaining whole wheat flour, ½ cup at a time; knead until dough begins to form a ball. Knead 6 to 8 minutes or until dough is smooth and elastic.

4. Place dough in greased bowl; turn to grease top. Cover and let rise in warm place 1½ to 2 hours or until doubled in size.

5. Spray two 9×5-inch loaf pans with nonstick cooking spray. Punch down dough. Divide dough in half; shape each half into loaf. Place in prepared pans. Cover and let rise in warm place 1 hour or until almost doubled in size.

6. Preheat oven to 375°F. Beat egg white and water in small bowl. Brush over tops of loaves; sprinkle with remaining ¼ cup oats.

7. Bake 35 to 45 minutes or until loaves sound hollow when tapped. Cool in pans 10 minutes; remove to wire rack to cool completely.

BACON CHEDDAR MONKEY BREAD

12 ounces bacon, cooked and chopped (about 1 cup)

1¾ cups (7 ounces) shredded sharp Cheddar cheese

¼ cup finely chopped green onions

2¾ to 3 cups all-purpose flour, divided

1 package (¼ ounce) rapid-rise active dry yeast

1 teaspoon salt

1 cup warm water (120°F)

2 tablespoons olive oil

⅓ cup butter, melted

1 egg

Makes 12 servings

1. Combine bacon, Cheddar and green onions in medium bowl; mix well.

2. Whisk 1½ cups flour, yeast, and salt in large bowl of stand mixer. Add warm water and oil; beat at medium speed with paddle attachment 3 minutes.

3. Replace paddle attachment with dough hook. Add 1¼ cups flour; knead at medium-low speed to make soft dough. Add 1 cup bacon mixture; knead 6 to 8 minutes or until dough is smooth and elastic. Add remaining flour, 1 tablespoon at a time, if necessary to clean side of bowl.

4. Shape dough into a ball. Place dough in greased bowl; turn to grease top. Cover and let rise in warm place about 30 minutes or until doubled in size.

5. Generously spray 12-cup (10-inch) bundt pan with nonstick cooking spray. Beat butter and egg in shallow bowl until blended.

6. Punch down dough. Roll golf-ball size pieces of dough (about 1½ inches) into balls. Dip balls in butter mixture; roll in remaining bacon mixture to coat. Layer balls in prepared pan. Cover and let rise in warm place about 40 minutes or until almost doubled in size. Preheat oven to 375°F.

7. Bake about 35 minutes or until golden brown. Loosen edges of bread with knife; invert onto wire rack. Cool 5 minutes; serve warm.

GOOD MORNING BREAD

1 **cup mashed ripe bananas (about 3 medium)**

¼ **cup warm milk (130°F)**

3 **tablespoons vegetable or canola oil**

1½ **to 2 cups bread flour, divided**

¾ **cup whole wheat flour**

½ **cup old-fashioned oats**

1 **package (¼ ounce) rapid-rise active dry yeast**

1 **teaspoon salt**

1 **teaspoon grated orange peel**

1 **teaspoon ground cinnamon**

Makes 1 loaf

1. Combine bananas, milk and oil in medium bowl; mix well. Whisk ½ cup bread flour, whole wheat flour, oats, yeast, salt, orange peel and cinnamon in large bowl of stand mixer. Add banana mixture; beat at medium speed with paddle attachment 3 minutes.

2. Replace paddle attachment with dough hook. Add enough remaining bread flour, ¼ cup at a time, to make soft dough. Knead at medium-low speed 5 minutes or until dough is smooth and elastic.

3. Shape dough into a ball. Place dough in greased bowl; turn to grease top. Cover and let rise in warm place about 40 minutes or until doubled in size.

4. Spray 9×5-inch loaf pan with nonstick cooking spray. Punch down dough. Shape into loaf; place in prepared pan. Cover and let rise in warm place about 30 minutes or until doubled in size. Preheat oven to 375°F.

5. Bake about 30 to 35 minutes or until golden brown and loaf sounds hollow when tapped. Remove to wire rack to cool completely.

PESTO-PARMESAN TWISTS

3 cups all-purpose flour

1 package (¼ ounce) rapid-rise active dry yeast

1½ teaspoons salt

3 tablespoons olive oil, divided

1 cup plus 2 tablespoons warm water (120°F)

⅓ cup pesto

¾ cup grated Parmesan cheese, divided

Makes 24 breadsticks

1. Combine flour, yeast and salt in food processor; pulse several times to mix. With motor running, add 2 tablespoons oil and warm water; process about 1 minute or until dough forms a rough ball that cleans side of bowl. Let rest 2 minutes; process 1 minute.

2. Shape dough into a ball. Place dough in greased bowl; turn to grease top. Cover and let rise in warm place about 30 minutes or until doubled in size.

3. Line two baking sheets with parchment paper. Punch down dough. Roll out dough into 20×10-inch rectangle on lightly floured surface.

4. Starting from short side, spread pesto evenly over half of dough; sprinkle with ½ cup Parmesan. Fold remaining half of dough over filling, forming 10-inch square. Roll square into 12×10-inch rectangle. Cut into 12 (1-inch) strips with sharp knife. Cut strips in half crosswise to form 24 strips total.

5. Twist each strip several times; place on prepared baking sheets. Cover and let rise in warm place 20 minutes. Preheat oven to 350°F.

6. Brush breadsticks with remaining 1 tablespoon oil; sprinkle with remaining ¼ cup Parmesan. Bake about 20 minutes or until golden brown. Serve warm.

ASIAGO-PEPPER LOAF

2½ to 3 cups bread flour or all-purpose flour, divided

¼ cup yellow cornmeal

1 package (¼ ounce) active dry yeast

2 teaspoons coarsely ground black pepper

1 teaspoon salt

1 cup warm water (110° to 115°F)

1 tablespoon canola oil

1 cup (4 ounces) shredded Asiago cheese

1 egg white

1 tablespoon water

Makes 1 loaf

1. Whisk 1 cup flour, cornmeal, yeast, pepper and salt in large bowl of stand mixer. Add warm water and oil; beat at low speed with paddle attachment 30 seconds. Beat at medium speed 5 minutes. Add Asiago and ½ cup flour; beat until blended.

2. Replace paddle attachment with dough hook. Add enough remaining flour, ¼ cup at a time, to make soft dough. Knead at low speed about 5 minutes or until dough is smooth and elastic.

3. Shape dough into a ball. Place in dough in greased bowl; turn to grease top. Cover and let rise in warm place about 1 hour 15 minutes or until doubled in size.

4. Punch down dough; turn out onto lightly floured surface. Cover and let rest 10 minutes. Line baking sheet with parchment paper.

5. Roll out dough into 15×7-inch rectangle. Starting with long side, roll up jelly-roll style. Pinch seam to seal; slightly stretch ends to taper. Place on prepared baking sheet.

6. Whisk egg white and 1 tablespoon water in small bowl; brush over top of loaf. Cover loosely and let rise in warm place about 45 minutes or until almost doubled in size.

7. Preheat oven to 350°F. Use sharp knife to make four shallow diagonal cuts in top of loaf.

8. Bake 20 minutes. Brush top of loaf with some of remaining egg white mixture. Bake 15 to 20 minutes or until loaf sounds hollow when tapped. Remove to wire rack to cool. Serve warm.

BEER PRETZEL ROLLS

1¼ cups lager or pale ale,
   at room temperature

3 tablespoons packed
   brown sugar

2 tablespoons milk

2 tablespoons butter, melted

1 package (¼ ounce) rapid-
   rise active dry yeast

3 to 4 cups bread flour, divided

2 teaspoons salt

4 quarts water

½ cup baking soda

2 teaspoons coarse salt

Makes 12 rolls

1. Combine lager, brown sugar, milk, butter and yeast in large bowl of stand mixer. Add 1 cup flour and 2 teaspoons salt; beat at low speed with paddle attachment 2 minutes.

2. Replace paddle attachment with dough hook. Add enough remaining flour, ½ cup at a time, to make stiff dough that cleans side of bowl. Knead at low speed about 5 minutes or until dough is smooth and elastic.

3. Shape dough into a ball. Place dough in greased bowl; turn to grease top. Cover and let rise in warm place 1 hour or until doubled in size.

4. Turn out dough onto lightly floured surface; knead several times. Divide dough into 12 pieces; shape each piece into a smooth ball by gently pulling top surface to underside and pinching bottom to seal. Place on ungreased baking sheet. Cover and let rise in warm place 30 minutes or until doubled in size.

5. Position oven rack in center of oven. Preheat oven to 425°F. Line second baking sheet with parchment paper.

6. Bring water and baking soda to a boil in large saucepan over medium-high heat. Add rolls to water, a few at a time; cook until puffed, turning once. Drain rolls on clean kitchen towel; place 2 inches apart on prepared baking sheet. Cut 1½-inch "X" in top of each roll with kitchen scissors. Sprinkle with coarse salt.

7. Bake 15 to 18 minutes or until crisp and golden brown. Remove to wire rack to cool completely.

SWEET YEAST BREADS

ORANGE POPPY SEED SWEET ROLLS

2¼ to 2¾ cups bread flour, divided

¼ cup granulated sugar

1 tablespoon poppy seeds

1 package (¼ ounce) rapid-rise active dry yeast

1 teaspoon salt

¾ cup plus 1½ tablespoons orange juice, at room temperature, divided

5 tablespoons butter, softened, divided

1 egg, beaten

1 cup powdered sugar

2 teaspoons grated orange peel

Makes 12 rolls

1. Whisk 1½ cups flour, granulated sugar, poppy seeds, yeast and salt in large bowl of stand mixer. Add ¾ cup orange juice, 4 tablespoons butter and egg; beat at medium speed with paddle attachment 3 minutes.

2. Replace paddle attachment with dough hook. Add enough remaining flour, ¼ cup at a time, to make soft dough. Knead at medium-low speed 5 minutes or until smooth and elastic. Shape dough into a ball. Place dough in greased bowl; turn to grease top. Cover and let rise in warm place about 40 minutes or until almost doubled in size.

3. Spray 13×9-inch baking pan with nonstick cooking spray. Punch down dough. Divide dough into 12 pieces; roll each piece into 10-inch rope. Coil ropes and tuck ends under. Place in prepared pan.

4. Melt remaining 1 tablespoon butter; brush over rolls. Cover and let rise in warm place 40 minutes. Preheat oven to 350°F.

5. Bake 20 minutes or until golden brown. Cool in pan on wire rack 10 minutes.

6. For glaze, whisk powdered sugar, remaining 1½ tablespoons orange juice and orange peel in small bowl until smooth. Spread glaze over warm rolls.

JELLY DOUGHNUT BITES

1¼ teaspoons active dry yeast

½ cup plus 3 tablespoons warm milk (95° to 105°F), divided

⅓ cup granulated sugar

1 tablespoon butter, softened

2½ to 2¾ cups all-purpose flour

1 egg

½ teaspoon salt

½ cup raspberry jam

Powdered sugar

Makes 48 doughnut bites

1. Dissolve yeast in 3 tablespoons warm milk in large bowl of stand mixer; let stand 5 minutes or until bubbly. Add granulated sugar, butter and remaining ½ cup milk; beat at medium speed with paddle attachment until blended.

2. Replace paddle attachment with dough hook. Add 2¼ cups flour, egg and salt; beat at low speed until dough starts to climb up dough hook. Add enough remaining flour, 1 tablespoon at a time, if necessary to prevent sticking. Knead at low speed 3 minutes or until dough is smooth and elastic.

3. Shape dough into a ball. Place dough in greased bowl; turn to grease top. Cover and let rise in warm place 1 hour or until doubled in size.

4. Spray 48 mini (1¾-inch) muffin cups with nonstick cooking spray. Punch down dough. Shape pieces of dough into 1-inch balls; place in prepared muffin cups. Cover and let rise 1 hour. Preheat oven to 375°F.

5. Bake 10 to 12 minutes or until light golden brown. Remove to wire racks to cool completely.

6. Place jam in pastry bag fitted with small round tip. Insert tip into side of each doughnut; squeeze about 1 teaspoon jam into center. Sprinkle filled doughnuts with powdered sugar.

Tip: These doughnuts are best eaten the same day they are made. They can be served warm or at room temperature. If desired, microwave on HIGH 10 seconds just before serving.

DATE-NUT BANANA BRAID

⅓ cup milk

2 tablespoons butter

1¾ to 2 cups bread flour, divided

¼ cup plus 1 tablespoon sugar, divided

1 package (¼ ounce) rapid-rise active dry yeast

¾ teaspoon salt

½ cup mashed ripe banana (about 1 large)

1 egg, beaten

½ cup chopped pitted dates

½ cup chopped walnuts

Makes 1 loaf

1. Combine milk and butter in small saucepan; heat over medium heat to 130°F. Whisk 1 cup flour, ¼ cup sugar, yeast and salt in large bowl of stand mixer. Add milk mixture, banana and egg; beat at medium speed with paddle attachment 3 minutes.

2. Replace paddle attachment with dough hook. Add dates, walnuts and enough remaining flour, ¼ cup at a time, to make soft dough. Knead at medium-low speed 5 to 7 minutes or until dough is smooth and elastic.

3. Shape dough into a ball. Place dough in greased bowl; turn to grease top. Cover and let rise in warm place about 45 minutes or until doubled in size.

4. Line baking sheet with parchment paper. Punch down dough. Divide dough into three pieces; roll each piece into 14-inch rope on lightly floured surface. Place ropes on prepared baking sheet; braid ropes and pinch ends to seal. Cover and let rise in warm place about 45 minutes or until doubled in size. Preheat oven to 375°F. Sprinkle loaf with remaining 1 tablespoon sugar.

5. Bake about 30 minutes or until golden brown. Remove to wire rack to cool completely.

RASPBERRY BREAKFAST RING

½ **cup warm milk (105° to 115°F)**

⅓ **cup warm water (105° to 115°F)**

1 **package (¼ ounce) active dry yeast**

3 to 3¼ **cups all-purpose flour, divided**

1 **egg**

3 **tablespoons butter, melted**

3 **tablespoons granulated sugar**

1 **teaspoon salt**

½ **cup raspberry preserves or fruit spread**

1 **teaspoon grated orange peel**

½ **cup plus 1 tablespoon sliced almonds, divided**

Powdered sugar

Makes 1 coffeecake

1. Combine warm milk and water in large bowl of stand mixer. Stir in yeast; let stand 5 minutes or until bubbly. Add 2¾ cups flour, egg, butter, granulated sugar and salt; beat at low speed with paddle attachment until soft dough forms.

2. Replace paddle attachment with dough hook. Add enough remaining flour, 1 tablespoon at a time, if necessary to prevent sticking. Knead at low speed 5 minutes or until dough is smooth and elastic. Place in dough in greased bowl; turn to grease top. Cover loosely and let rise in warm place 45 minutes to 1 hour or until doubled in size.

3. Punch down dough. Cover and let rest in warm place 10 minutes. Line baking sheet with parchment paper.

4. Roll out dough into 16×9-inch rectangle on lightly floured surface. Combine preserves and orange peel in small bowl; spread over dough. Sprinkle with almonds. Starting with long side, roll up dough jelly-roll style; pinch seam to seal. Shape dough into ring on prepared baking sheet, keeping seam side down and pinching ends together.

5. Use serrated knife to cut dough at 1-inch intervals to within ¾ inch of center. Gently lift each section and turn it on its side, overlapping slices. Cover loosely and let rise in warm place 30 to 45 minutes or until doubled in size. Preheat oven to 350°F. Sprinkle with remaining 1 tablespoon almonds.

6. Bake about 25 minutes or until golden brown. Remove to wire rack to cool completely.

7. Sprinkle with powdered sugar just before serving.

HOT CROSS BUNS

1 package (¼ ounce) active
   dry yeast
1 cup warm milk (105° to
   115°F), divided
2¼ cups all-purpose flour
1 cup currants
½ cup whole wheat flour
¼ cup granulated sugar
¼ teaspoon salt
¼ teaspoon ground nutmeg
2 eggs
¼ cup (½ stick) butter, melted
½ cup powdered sugar
1 to 2 tablespoons milk or
   cream

Makes 12 buns

1. Dissolve yeast in ¼ cup warm milk in small bowl; let stand 10 minutes or until bubbly.

2. Combine all-purpose flour, currants, whole wheat flour, granulated sugar, salt and nutmeg in medium bowl. Beat eggs, butter and remaining ¾ cup warm milk in large bowl of stand mixer.

3. Add yeast mixture to egg mixture. Gradually add flour mixture; beat at medium speed with paddle attachment until well blended. (Dough will be sticky.) Cover and let rise in warm place 1 hour or until doubled in size.

4. Preheat oven to 400°F. Spray 12 standard (2½-inch) muffin cups with nonstick cooking spray. Vigorously stir down dough with wooden spoon. Spoon about ¼ cup dough into each muffin cup; smooth tops.

5. Bake 20 minutes or until golden brown. Cool in pan 5 minutes; remove to wire rack to cool completely.

6. For icing, whisk powdered sugar and 1 tablespoon milk in small bowl until smooth. Add remaining milk, if necessary, to reach desired consistency. Spoon into small resealable food storage bag. Cut off small corner of bag; pipe cross on center of each bun.

MINI COCONUT ORANGE ROLLS

¾ **cup plus 2 tablespoons milk**

⅓ **cup plus 2 tablespoons butter, divided**

2 **to 2¼ cups bread flour, divided**

½ **cup plus ⅓ cup sugar, divided**

1 **package (¼ ounce) rapid-rise active dry yeast**

1 **tablespoon grated orange peel, divided**

¾ **teaspoon salt**

½ **cup flaked coconut**

⅓ **cup orange juice**

2 **tablespoons light corn syrup**

Makes 24 rolls

1. Combine milk and ⅓ cup butter in small saucepan; heat over medium heat to 120°F (butter does not need to melt completely). Whisk 1 cup flour, ¼ cup sugar, yeast, 1 teaspoon grated orange peel and salt in large bowl of stand mixer. Add milk mixture; beat at medium speed with paddle attachment 2 minutes.

2. Replace paddle attachment with dough hook. Add enough remaining flour, ¼ cup at a time, to make firm dough. Knead at medium-low speed 5 minutes or until smooth and elastic.

3. Shape dough into a ball. Place dough in greased bowl; turn to grease top. Cover and let rise in warm place about 40 minutes or until doubled in size.

4. Spray 24 mini (1¾-inch) muffin cups with nonstick cooking spray. Combine ¼ cup sugar and remaining 2 teaspoons grated orange peel in small bowl. Divide dough in half; roll out each half into 12×6-inch rectangle on lightly floured surface. Melt remaining 2 tablespoons butter; spread 1 tablespoon butter over each rectangle. Sprinkle each with half of sugar mixture and half of coconut. Starting with long sides, roll up tightly jelly-roll style; pinch seams to seal. Cut crosswise into 1-inch slices; place slices, cut sides up, in prepared muffin cups. Cover and let rise in warm place about 30 minutes or until doubled in size. Preheat oven to 375°F.

5. Bake about 25 minutes or until golden brown. Remove to wire racks to cool 5 minutes.

6. Meanwhile, combine remaining ⅓ cup sugar, orange juice and corn syrup in small saucepan; bring to a boil over high heat. Reduce heat to low; simmer 5 minutes. Brush over warm rolls.

PECAN-CINNAMON STICKY BUNS

3 to 3½ cups all-purpose flour

⅓ cup nonfat dry milk powder

1 package (¼ ounce) rapid-rise active dry yeast

1 teaspoon salt

1 cup water

2 tablespoons honey, divided

1 egg, beaten

½ cup (1 stick) plus 5 tablespoons butter, melted, divided

¾ cup packed brown sugar, divided

3 tablespoons light corn syrup

¾ cup chopped pecans

2 teaspoons ground cinnamon

Makes 12 buns

1. Whisk 3 cups flour, milk powder, yeast and salt in large bowl of stand mixer. Combine water and honey in small saucepan; heat over medium heat to 120°F, stirring to dissolve honey. Add to flour mixture; beat with paddle attachment at low speed until blended. Beat in egg and 3 tablespoons melted butter until soft dough forms.

2. Replace paddle attachment with dough hook. Add enough remaining flour, 1 tablespoon at a time, if necessary to prevent sticking. Knead at low speed 5 minutes or until dough is smooth and elastic.

3. Shape dough into a ball. Place dough in greased bowl; turn to grease top. Cover and let rise in warm place 30 to 40 minutes or until doubled in size.

4. Meanwhile, combine ½ cup butter, ½ cup brown sugar and corn syrup in small saucepan; cook and stir over medium heat until melted and smooth. Pour into bottom of 9-inch round cake pan; sprinkle with pecans. Combine remaining ¼ cup brown sugar and cinnamon in small bowl.

5. Punch down dough. Roll out dough into 15×9-inch rectangle on floured surface. Brush with remaining 2 tablespoons butter; sprinkle with cinnamon-sugar. Starting with long side, roll up dough jelly-roll style; pinch seam to seal. Cut crosswise into 12 (1¼-inch) slices; arrange slices cut sides up in prepared pan. Cover and let rise in warm place 25 minutes. Preheat oven to 350°F.

6. Bake 30 minutes or until golden brown. Cool in pan 2 minutes; invert onto plate.

BAKED DOUGHNUTS
WITH CINNAMON GLAZE

  2 **cups milk, divided**

  ½ **cup (1 stick) butter**

  5 **to 5½ cups all-purpose flour, divided**

  ⅔ **cup granulated sugar**

  2 **packages (¼ ounce each) active dry yeast**

  1 **teaspoon salt**

  1 **teaspoon grated lemon peel**

  ½ **teaspoon ground nutmeg**

  2 **eggs**

  2 **cups sifted powdered sugar**

  ½ **teaspoon ground cinnamon**

Makes 24 doughnuts and holes

1. Combine 1¾ cups milk and butter in small saucepan; heat to 120° to 130°F (butter does not need to melt completely). Combine 2 cups flour, granulated sugar, yeast, salt, lemon peel and nutmeg in large bowl of stand mixer. Gradually add milk mixture; beat at low speed with paddle attachment until blended. Beat at medium speed 2 minutes. Beat in eggs and 1 cup flour at low speed. Beat at medium speed 2 minutes.

2. Beat in enough additional flour, about 2 cups, at low speed to make soft dough. Shape dough into a ball. Place dough in greased bowl; turn to grease top. Cover and refrigerate at least 2 hours or up to 24 hours.

3. Punch down dough; turn out onto lightly floured surface. Knead about 1 minute or until no longer sticky. Add enough remaining flour, 1 tablespoon at a time, if necessary to prevent sticking.

4. Line two baking sheets with parchment paper. Roll out dough to ½-inch thickness with lightly floured rolling pin. Cut out dough with floured 2½-inch doughnut cutter. Reroll scraps, reserving doughnut holes. Place doughnuts and holes 2 inches apart on prepared baking sheets. Cover and let rise in warm place about 30 minutes or until doubled in size.

5. For glaze, combine powdered sugar and cinnamon in small bowl. Stir in remaining milk, 1 tablespoon at a time, until glaze reaches desired consistency. Preheat oven to 400°F.

6. Bake doughnuts and holes 8 to 10 minutes or until golden brown. Remove to wire racks; cool 5 minutes. Place waxed paper under racks. Dip warm doughnuts into glaze; return to racks to set. Serve warm.

HONEY-PECAN COFFEECAKE

⅔ cup milk

6 tablespoons (¾ stick) butter, softened

9 tablespoons honey, divided

2½ to 3½ cups all-purpose flour, divided

1 package (¼ ounce) active dry yeast

¾ teaspoon salt

3 eggs, divided

1¼ cups coarsely chopped pecans, toasted,* divided

3 tablespoons packed brown sugar

1½ tablespoons butter, melted

1 tablespoon ground cinnamon

1 teaspoon water

*To toast pecans, spread in single layer on baking sheet. Toast in preheated 350°F oven 8 to 10 minutes or until browned, stirring frequently.

Makes 1 coffeecake

1. Combine milk, softened butter and 3 tablespoons honey in small saucepan; heat to 120° to 130°F. Whisk 2¼ cups flour, yeast and salt in large bowl of stand mixer. Gradually add milk mixture; beat at medium speed with paddle attachment until blended. Beat 2 eggs in small bowl; add to flour mixture and beat 2 minutes or until well blended.

2. Replace paddle attachment with dough hook. Add enough remaining flour, 1 tablespoon at a time, to make soft but rough dough. Knead at low speed about 5 minutes or until dough is smooth and elastic, adding additional flour if necessary to prevent sticking.

3. Shape dough into a ball. Place dough in greased bowl; turn to grease top. Cover and let rise in warm place 35 minutes or until dough has increased in size by one third. Punch down dough. Roll out dough into 14×8-inch rectangle on lightly floured surface with lightly floured rolling pin.

4. Combine 1 cup pecans, brown sugar, melted butter, cinnamon and 3 tablespoons honey in small bowl. Spread evenly over dough; press in gently with fingertips. Starting with long side, roll up tightly jelly-roll style; pinch seam to seal. Turn seam side down and flatten slightly. Twist dough six to eight turns.

5. Spray 9-inch round cake pan with nonstick cooking spray. Place dough in pan in loose spiral, starting in center and working outward. Tuck outside end under dough; pinch to seal. Cover loosely and let rise in warm place about 1 hour or until doubled in size.

6. Preheat oven to 375°F. Place cake pan on baking sheet. Beat remaining egg and 1 teaspoon water in small bowl; brush over dough. Drizzle with remaining 3 tablespoons honey; sprinkle with remaining ¼ cup pecans.

7. Bake 40 to 45 minutes or until deep golden brown. Rotate pan and tent with foil halfway through baking time to prevent burning. Remove foil for last 5 minutes of baking. Cool in pan on wire rack 5 minutes; remove to wire rack to cool completely.

CINNAMON ROLLS

1 package (¼ ounce) active
  dry yeast

¼ cup warm water
  (100° to 110°F)

½ cup plus 2 tablespoons milk,
  divided

¼ cup granulated sugar

5 tablespoons butter, melted,
  divided

1 egg

1 teaspoon vanilla

½ teaspoon salt

2½ to 2¾ cups all-purpose flour,
  divided

½ cup packed brown sugar

1 tablespoon ground
  cinnamon

⅓ cup raisins (optional)

½ cup powdered sugar, sifted

Makes 18 rolls

1. Dissolve yeast in warm water in large bowl of stand mixer; let stand 5 minutes or until bubbly.

2. Add ½ cup milk, granulated sugar, 2 tablespoons butter, egg, vanilla and salt; beat at medium speed with paddle attachment until blended. Add 2½ cups flour; beat until soft dough forms.

3. Replace paddle attachment with dough hook. Add enough remaining flour, 1 tablespoon at a time, if necessary to prevent sticking. Knead at low speed 5 minutes or until dough is smooth and elastic.

4. Shape dough into a ball. Place dough in greased bowl; turn to grease top. Cover and let rise in warm place about 1 hour or until doubled in size.

5. Spray two 8-inch round cake pans with nonstick cooking spray. Combine brown sugar, 1 tablespoon butter and cinnamon in small bowl.

6. Punch down dough. Roll out dough into 18×8-inch rectangle on lightly floured surface. Brush with remaining 2 tablespoons butter; spread with brown sugar mixture. Sprinkle with raisins, if desired. Starting with long side, roll up dough jelly-roll style; pinch seam to seal. Cut crosswise into 1-inch slices; arrange slices cut sides up in prepared pans. Cover loosely and let rise in warm place 30 to 40 minutes or until almost doubled in size. Preheat oven to 350°F.

7. Bake 18 minutes or until golden brown. Remove to wire racks to cool slightly.

8. For glaze, whisk powdered sugar and 1 tablespoon milk in small bowl until smooth. Add additional milk if necessary to reach desired consistency. Drizzle glaze over warm rolls.

CHERRY, ALMOND AND CHOCOLATE TWIST

1 **cup cold water**

1 **cup dried sweet or sour cherries**

½ **cup sugar, divided**

1 **package (¼ ounce) active dry yeast**

¼ **cup warm water (105° to 115°F)**

½ **cup plus 1 tablespoon milk, divided**

3 **tablespoons butter, cut into pieces**

2 **eggs, divided**

1 **tablespoon grated lemon peel**

½ **teaspoon salt**

½ **teaspoon almond extract**

2½ **to 2¾ cups all-purpose flour**

½ **cup canned almond filling (about 12 ounces)**

¾ **cup semisweet chocolate chips**

Almond Glaze (recipe follows)

Makes 1 coffeecake

1. Combine cold water, cherries and ¼ cup sugar in small saucepan; bring to a boil over high heat, stirring constantly. Remove from heat; cover and set aside.

2. Dissolve yeast in ¼ cup warm water in large bowl of stand mixer; let stand 5 minutes or until bubbly.

3. Meanwhile, heat ½ cup milk and butter in medium saucepan over high heat until milk bubbles around edge of saucepan, stirring constantly (butter does not need to melt completely). Remove from heat; stir occasionally until milk is warm to touch.

4. Add milk mixture, remaining ¼ cup sugar, 1 egg, lemon peel, salt and almond extract to yeast mixture; beat at medium speed with paddle attchment until well blended. Add 2¼ cups flour; beat at low speed until dough forms a sticky ball. Stir in enough remaining flour to make soft dough.

5. Replace paddle attachment with dough hook. Add enough remaining flour, 1 tablespoon at a time, if necessary to prevent sticking. Knead at low speed 5 minutes or until dough is smooth and elastic. Shape dough into a ball. Place dough in greased bowl; turn to grease top. Cover and let rise in warm place 1 to 2 hours or until doubled in size.

6. Preheat oven to 350°F. Line large baking sheet with parchment paper. Punch down dough several times. Turn out dough onto lightly floured surface; knead dough 10 to 12 times or until smooth. Shape dough into 10-inch log, flatten slightly. Roll out dough into 18×8-inch rectangle with lightly floured rolling pin.

7. Drain cherries. Spread almond filling evenly over dough; sprinkle with cherries and chocolate chips. Starting with long side, roll up dough jelly-roll style; pinch seam to seal.

8. Transfer roll to prepared baking sheet. Use long sharp knife to cut roll in half lengthwise (through all layers). Turn halves cut sides up on baking sheet; carefully twist halves together, keeping cut sides facing up as much as possible. Press ends together to seal and tuck underneath.

9. Beat remaining egg and 1 tablespoon milk in small bowl; brush lightly over dough.

10. Bake 30 minutes or until golden brown. (If coffeecake browns too quickly, cover loosely with foil.) Cool on baking sheet 5 minutes; remove to wire rack to cool completely. Prepare Almond Glaze; drizzle over coffeecake. Let stand until set.

Almond Glaze: Whisk ½ cup powdered sugar, sifted, 2 teaspoons milk and ¼ teaspoon almond extract in small bowl until smooth. Add additional milk if necessary to reach desired consistency.

GINGER-PEACH BLOSSOMS

1 can (16 ounces) sliced peaches in light syrup, divided

3 tablespoons milk

3 tablespoons butter

2¾ cups all-purpose flour, divided

¼ cup plus 2 tablespoons granulated sugar, divided

¼ cup packed brown sugar

1 package (¼ ounce) rapid-rise active dry yeast

1¾ teaspoons ground ginger, divided

1⅛ teaspoons ground cinnamon, divided

1 teaspoon salt

⅛ teaspoon ground nutmeg

⅛ teaspoon ground cloves

2 eggs, divided

Makes 12 rolls

1. Drain peaches, reserving ¼ cup syrup Coarsely chop peaches. Combine reserved ¼ cup peach syrup, milk and butter in small saucepan; heat over medium heat to 120°F.

2. Whisk 1 cup flour, ¼ cup granulated sugar, brown sugar, yeast, 1½ teaspoons ginger, 1 teaspoon cinnamon, salt, nutmeg and cloves in large bowl of stand mixer. Add milk mixture and 1 egg; beat at medium speed with paddle attachment 3 minutes.

3. Replace paddle attachment with dough hook. Add ½ cup chopped peaches and enough remaining flour, ¼ cup at a time, to make soft dough. Knead at medium-low speed 5 minutes or until smooth and elastic. Shape dough into a ball. Place dough in greased bowl; turn to grease top. Cover and let rise in warm place 45 minutes or until doubled in size.

4. Line two baking sheets with parchment paper. Punch down dough. Divide dough into 12 pieces; shape into balls. Place 2 inches apart on prepared baking sheets. Cover and let rise in warm place about 45 minutes or until doubled in size. Preheat oven to 350°F.

5. Combine remaining chopped peaches, ¼ teaspoon ginger, ⅛ teaspoon cinnamon and 1 tablespoon granulated sugar in medium bowl. Make indentation in center of each roll; spoon heaping teaspoon peach mixture into each indentation. Use kitchen scissors to make five cuts from edge to center of each roll to form petals. Beat remaining egg; brush over dough. Sprinkle with remaining 1 tablespoon granulated sugar.

6. Bake about 18 minutes or until golden brown. Remove to wire racks to cool slightly. Serve warm or cool completely.

CINNAMON-NUT BUBBLE RING

¾ cup plus 1½ tablespoons milk, divided

5 tablespoons butter, divided

1¾ to 2 cups bread flour, divided

¾ cup granulated sugar, divided

1 package (¼ ounce) rapid-rise active dry yeast

1 teaspoon salt

4½ teaspoons ground cinnamon, divided

1 egg

½ cup finely chopped walnuts

1 cup powdered sugar

Makes 1 coffeecake

1. Combine ¾ cup milk and 2 tablespoons butter in small saucepan; heat over medium heat to 120°F. Whisk 1 cup flour, ¼ cup granulated sugar, yeast, salt and ½ teaspoon cinnamon in large bowl of stand mixer. Add milk mixture and egg; beat at medium speed with paddle attachment 3 minutes.

2. Replace paddle attachment with dough hook. Add walnuts and enough remaining flour, ¼ cup at a time, to make soft dough. Knead at medium-low speed 5 minutes or until smooth and elastic.

3. Shape dough into a ball. Place dough in greased bowl; turn to grease top. Cover and let rise in warm place about 45 minutes or until doubled in size.

4. Spray 10-inch tube pan with nonstick cooking spray. Melt remaining 3 tablespoons butter in shallow bowl. Combine remaining ½ cup granulated sugar and 4 teaspoons cinnamon in another shallow bowl.

5. Punch down dough. Roll pieces of dough into 2-inch balls. Roll balls in melted butter; coat with cinnamon-sugar. Arrange in prepared pan; cover and let rise about 45 minutes or until doubled in size. Preheat oven to 350°F.

6. Bake 30 minutes or until golden brown. Cool in pan on wire rack 10 minutes; remove to wire rack.

7. For glaze, whisk powdered sugar and remaining 1½ tablespoons milk in small bowl until smooth. Drizzle glaze over coffeecake.

PIZZA & FLATBREADS

TOMATO AND CHEESE FOCACCIA

1 package (¼ ounce) active
   dry yeast

¾ cup warm water
   (105° to 115°F)

2 cups all-purpose flour

½ teaspoon salt

4 tablespoons plus 1 teaspoon
   olive oil, divided

1 teaspoon dried Italian
   seasoning

8 oil-packed sun-dried
   tomatoes, well drained

½ cup (2 ounces) shredded
   provolone cheese

¼ cup grated Parmesan cheese

Makes 1 (10-inch) bread

1. Dissolve yeast in warm water in small bowl; let stand 5 minutes or until bubbly. Combine flour and salt in food processor. Add yeast mixture and 3 tablespoons oil; process until mixture forms a ball. Process 1 minute.

2. Turn out dough onto lightly floured surface. Knead about 2 minutes or until smooth and elastic. Place dough in greased bowl; turn to grease top. Cover and let rise in warm place about 30 minutes or until doubled in size.

3. Brush 10-inch round cake pan, deep-dish pizza pan or springform pan with 1 teaspoon oil. Punch down dough; let rest 5 minutes.

4. Press dough into prepared pan. Brush with remaining 1 tablespoon oil; sprinkle with Italian seasoning. Press sun-dried tomatoes into top of dough; sprinkle with cheeses. Cover and let rise in warm place 15 minutes. Preheat oven to 425°F.

5. Bake 20 to 25 minutes or until golden brown. Cut into wedges.

Serving Suggestion: Serve with rosemary-infused olive oil for dipping.

NAAN (INDIAN FLATBREAD)

1 package (¼ ounce) active
 dry yeast

1 teaspoon sugar

¼ cup plus 2 tablespoons warm
 water, divided

3 cups all-purpose flour

1 teaspoon salt

1 teaspoon kalonji* seeds or
 poppy seeds (optional)

½ cup plain whole milk Greek
 yogurt

¼ cup (½ stick) melted butter,
 plus additional butter for
 brushing on naan

*Kalonji seed is often called onion seed or
black cumin seed. It is available in Indian
markets and is traditional in some varieties
of naan.

Makes 12 servings

1. Dissolve yeast and sugar in 2 tablespoons warm water in small bowl; let stand 5 minutes or until bubbly. Whisk flour, salt and kalonji, if desired, in large bowl of stand mixer. Attach dough hook; stir until blended.

2. Add yeast mixture, yogurt and ¼ cup butter; knead at low speed until blended. Add remaining ¼ cup water, 1 tablespoon at a time, until dough comes together and cleans side of bowl. (You may not need all the water.) Knead at low speed 5 to 7 minutes or until dough is smooth and elastic.

3. Shape dough into a ball. Place dough in greased bowl; turn to grease top. Cover and let rise in warm place 1½ to 2 hours or until doubled in size.

4. Punch down dough; divide into six pieces. Roll each piece into a ball; place on plate sprayed with nonstick cooking spray. Cover and let rest 10 to 15 minutes.

5. Meanwhile, prepare grill for direct cooking or preheat oven to 500°F with baking stone on rack in lower third of oven. (Remove other racks.)

6. Place each ball of dough on lightly floured surface; roll and stretch into ⅛-inch-thick oval. Place on grid or baking stone 2 or 3 at a time. Grill, covered, or bake 2 minutes until puffed. Turn, brush tops with butter and grill or bake 1 to 2 minutes until browned in patches on both sides. Brush bottoms with butter; serve warm.

PIZZA MARGHERITA

Crust

2 cups all-purpose flour

1 cup whole wheat flour

1 package (¼ ounce) rapid-
   rise active dry yeast

2 teaspoons salt

1 cup warm water (120°F)

2 tablespoons extra virgin
   olive oil

Sauce*

1 tablespoon olive oil

1 onion, chopped

2 cloves garlic, minced

1 can (about 14 ounces) fire-
   roasted diced tomatoes

⅓ cup red wine (optional)

½ teaspoon Italian seasoning

Toppings

Sliced plum tomatoes

Fresh mozzarella cheese,
   thinly sliced

Fresh basil, torn into pieces

*Or substitute prepared pizza sauce,
if desired.*

Makes 2 medium pizzas
(6 to 8 servings)

1. Combine all-purpose flour, whole wheat flour, yeast and salt in food processor; pulse just until combined. With motor running, add warm water and 2 tablespoons oil through feed tube; process 30 seconds or until dough forms a ball. Dough should be slightly sticky. If ball does not form and dough seems too wet, add additional all-purpose flour, 1 tablespoon at a time. If too dry, add water, 1 tablespoon at a time.

2. Turn out dough onto floured surface; knead 1 minute. Place dough in greased bowl; turn to grease top. Cover and let rise in warm place 45 minutes or until almost doubled in size.

3. For sauce, heat 1 tablespoon oil in medium saucepan over medium heat. Add onion and garlic; cook and stir 2 minutes or until softened. Add diced tomatoes, wine, if desired, and Italian seasoning; cook 5 to 10 minutes over medium-high heat or until slightly reduced, stirring occasionally. Remove from heat; let cool. Transfer to food processor; pulse until almost smooth. Refrigerate until ready to use.

4. Preheat oven to 450°F. Sprinkle two baking sheets or pizza pans with cornmeal. Punch down dough. Divide dough into two pieces; roll out each piece into 12-inch circle on floured surface with floured rolling pin. Place dough circles on prepared baking sheets. Spread with thin layer of sauce. (Freeze leftover sauce for later use.) Top with plum tomatoes and mozzarella.

5. Bake 6 to 10 minutes or until crust begins to brown around edges and toppings are bubbly. Remove to cutting board; sprinkle with basil.

ROSEMARY LAGER FOCACCIA

1¼ cups lager or other light-colored beer

4 tablespoons extra virgin olive oil, divided

1 package (¼ ounce) active dry yeast

1 tablespoon sugar

3¼ cups all-purpose flour, divided

2 teaspoons coarse salt, divided

¼ cup fresh rosemary leaves

Makes 12 servings

1. Place lager in medium microwavable bowl; microwave on HIGH 25 seconds. Stir in 3 tablespoons oil, yeast and sugar; let stand 5 minutes or until bubbly.

2. Whisk 3 cups flour and 1 teaspoon salt in large bowl of stand mixer. Add lager mixture; beat at medium-low speed with paddle attachment until dough begins to clean side of bowl.

3. Replace paddle attachment with dough hook. Add enough remaining flour, 1 tablespoon at a time, if necessary to clean side of bowl. Knead at low speed 5 to 7 minutes or until dough is almost smooth and elastic. (Dough will remain slightly sticky.)

4. Shape dough into a ball. Place in greased bowl; turn to grease top. Cover and let rise in warm place 1½ hours or until doubled in size.

5. Line baking sheet with parchment paper. Place dough on prepared baking sheet; stretch into 15×10-inch rectangle. Cover and let rise 30 minutes.

6. Preheat oven to 325°F. Brush dough with remaining 1 tablespoon oil; sprinkle with rosemary and remaining 1 teaspoon salt.

7. Bake 30 minutes or until golden brown. Remove to wire rack to cool 10 minutes. Serve warm or cool completely.

PITA (POCKET BREAD)

1 tablespoon sugar

1 package (¼ ounce) active
dry yeast

¾ to 1 cup warm water
(105° to 115°F), divided

2¾ cups all-purpose flour, plus
additional for baking sheet

1 teaspoon salt

1 teaspoon vegetable oil

Makes 8 pitas

1. Dissolve sugar and yeast in ¼ cup warm water in small bowl; let stand 5 minutes or until bubbly.

2. Combine flour, salt and oil in food processor; pulse to mix. Add yeast mixture; process about 10 seconds or until blended.

3. With motor running, slowly drizzle just enough water through feed tube so dough forms a ball that cleans side of bowl. Process until ball turns around bowl about 25 times. Turn off processor; let dough rest 1 to 2 minutes.

4. With motor running, slowly drizzle in enough remaining water to make dough soft, smooth and satiny but not sticky. Process until dough turns around bowl about 15 times.

5. Shape dough into a ball. Place dough in greased bowl; turn to grease top. Cover and let rise in warm place 45 minutes to 1 hour or until almost doubled in size.

6. Sprinkle baking sheet lightly with flour. Turn out dough onto lightly floured surface. Punch down dough; divide into eight pieces. Shape each piece into a smooth ball. Roll each ball into 6-inch circle and place on prepared baking sheet. Cover loosely and let rise in warm place about 45 minutes or until doubled in size. Preheat oven to 500°F.

7. Bake 5 to 7 minutes or until lightly browned and puffy. Remove to paper towels to cool.

WHOLE WHEAT TORTILLAS

1½ cups whole wheat flour

½ cup all-purpose flour

1 teaspoon baking powder

½ teaspoon salt

¼ cup shortening

½ cup warm water

Makes 8 large or 12 small tortillas

1. Combine whole wheat flour, all-purpose flour, baking powder and salt in medium bowl. Cut in shortening with pastry blender or two knives until mixture resembles fine crumbs.

2. Gradually add warm water; stir with fork until dough forms. Turn out onto lightly floured surface; knead 2 minutes or until smooth. Shape dough into a ball. Place dough in bowl; cover and let rest 30 minutes.

3. Divide dough into 8 pieces for 9-inch tortillas or 12 pieces for 6-inch tortillas. Keep dough covered to prevent it from drying out. Working with one piece at a time, roll out dough into ⅛-inch-thick circle on lightly floured surface.

4. Heat ungreased heavy skillet or griddle over medium-high heat. Cook tortillas 2 to 3 minutes per side or until bubbly and browned. Stack cooked tortillas in tightly covered dish or wrap in foil to keep soft. Serve warm.

Note: If desired, tortillas may be made ahead for later use. Cool tortillas; wrap well and refrigerate. To reheat, wrap with foil and heat in a preheated 350°F oven for 12 minutes.

PEPPERONI PIZZA

1 cup lager or pale ale,
  at room temperature

3 tablespoons olive oil

1 package (¼ ounce) rapid-
  rise active dry yeast

2¾ cups bread flour

1 teaspoon salt

6 ounces pepperoni slices
  (about 32 to 36)

1 cup prepared pizza sauce

2 cups (8 ounces) shredded
  mozzarella cheese

¼ cup grated Parmesan cheese

Makes 2 (10-inch) pizzas

1. Combine lager, oil and yeast in large bowl of stand mixer. Add 1 cup flour and salt; beat at medium speed with paddle attachment 2 minutes. Add enough remaining flour, ½ cup at a time, to make soft dough that cleans side of bowl.

2. Replace paddle attachment with dough hook. Knead at low speed 5 minutes or until dough is smooth and elastic.

3. Shape dough into a ball. Place in greased bowl; turn to grease top. Cover and let rise in warm place about 1 hour or until doubled in size.

4. Preheat oven to 425°F. Punch down dough; place on lightly floured surface. Divide dough in half; shape each half into a ball. Cover and let rest 10 minutes.

5. Roll out each ball into 10-inch circle; place on ungreased baking sheets. Spread ½ cup pizza sauce over each crust, leaving ½-inch border around edges. Top with pepperoni, mozzarella and Parmesan.

6. Bake 15 minutes or until crust is golden brown and cheese is bubbly. Let stand 3 minutes before serving.

ROASTED PEPPER AND OLIVE FOCACCIA

1 **package (¼ ounce) active dry yeast**

1 **teaspoon sugar**

1½ **cups warm water (105° to 110°F)**

4 **cups all-purpose flour, divided**

7 **tablespoons olive oil, divided**

1 **teaspoon salt**

¼ **cup roasted red peppers, drained and cut into strips**

¼ **cup pitted black olives**

Makes 12 servings

1. Dissove yeast and sugar in warm water in large bowl of stand mixer; let stand 5 minutes or until bubbly. Add 3½ cups flour, 3 tablespoons oil and salt; beat at medium-low speed with paddle attachment to make soft dough.

2. Replace paddle attachment with dough hook. Add remaining flour, 1 tablespoon at a time, if necessary to prevent sticking. Knead at low speed 5 minutes or until dough is smooth and elastic.

3. Shape dough into a ball. Place dough in greased bowl; turn to grease top. Cover and let rise in warm place 1 hour or until doubled in size.

4. Brush 15×10-inch jelly-roll pan with 1 tablespoon oil. Punch down dough. Turn out dough onto lightly floured surface. Flatten into rectangle; roll out almost to size of pan. Place dough in pan; gently press dough to edges.

5. Poke surface of dough with end of wooden spoon handle, making indentations every 1 or 2 inches. Brush with remaining 3 tablespoons oil; gently press roasted peppers and olives into dough. Cover and let rise in warm place 30 minutes or until doubled in size. Preheat oven to 450°F.

6. Bake 12 to 18 minutes or until golden brown. Cut into squares or rectangles. Serve warm.

NEAPOLITAN PIZZA

1 package (¼ ounce) active
   dry yeast

1 teaspoon sugar

½ to ¾ cup warm water
   (105° to 115°F), divided

2 cups all-purpose flour

1 tablespoon plus 1 teaspoon
   olive oil, divided

½ teaspoon salt

1 cup Pizza Sauce
   (recipe follows)

2 cups (8 ounces) shredded
   mozzarella cheese

4 ounces sliced pepperoni
   (about 1 cup)

1 small green bell pepper,
   seeded and sliced

1 small onion, peeled and
   sliced

⅓ cup grated Parmesan cheese

Makes 4 servings

1. Dissolve yeast and sugar in ¼ cup warm water in small bowl; let stand about 5 minutes or until bubbly.

2. Combine flour, 1 tablespoon oil and salt in food processor; process 5 seconds. Add yeast mixture; process 10 seconds or until blended.

3. With motor running, slowly drizzle just enough water through feed tube so dough forms a ball that cleans side of bowl. Process until ball turns around bowl about 25 times. Let dough rest 1 to 2 minutes.

4. With motor running, slowly drizzle in enough remaining water to make dough soft, smooth and satiny but not sticky. Process until dough turns around bowl about 15 times.

5. Brush 14-inch pizza pan or large baking sheet with remaining 1 teaspoon oil. Shape dough into a ball; place on prepared pan. Cover with inverted bowl or plastic wrap and let rest 10 minutes.

6. Meanwhile, prepare Pizza Sauce. Preheat oven to 425°F. Roll out or pat dough to cover pan, making slight ridge around edge. Spread sauce evenly over dough; top with mozzarella, pepperoni, bell pepper, onion and Parmesan.

7. Bake 15 to 20 minutes or until crust is golden brown.

Pizza Sauce: Place 3 peeled, seeded and quartered tomatoes in food processor; pulse 3 or 4 times to coarsely chop. Add 1 (8-ounce) can tomato sauce, 1½ teaspoons dried Italian seasoning or dried oregano, ½ teaspoon salt, ¼ teaspoon sugar and ⅛ teaspoon black pepper; pulse until blended.

SWEET QUICK BREADS

BLUEBERRY HILL BREAD

2 cups all-purpose flour

¾ cup packed brown sugar

2 teaspoons baking powder

1 teaspoon baking soda

1 teaspoon salt

½ teaspoon ground nutmeg

¾ cup buttermilk

1 egg

3 tablespoons vegetable oil
   or melted butter

1 cup fresh or thawed frozen
   blueberries

Makes 1 loaf

1. Preheat oven to 350°F. Spray 8×4-inch loaf pan with nonstick cooking spray.

2. Combine flour, brown sugar, baking powder, baking soda, salt and nutmeg in food processor; process 5 seconds. Whisk buttermilk, egg and oil in medium bowl until blended. Add to flour mixture; process 5 to 10 seconds or just until flour is moistened. (Do not overprocess. Batter should be lumpy.)

3. Sprinkle blueberries over batter; pulse just to mix blueberries into batter. (Batter will be stiff.) Pour batter into prepared pan.

4. Bake 50 to 60 minutes or until toothpick inserted into center comes out clean. Cool in pan on wire rack 15 minutes; remove to wire rack to cool completely.

APPLESAUCE SPICE BREAD

1½ cups all-purpose flour

1 cup unsweetened applesauce

¾ cup packed brown sugar

¼ cup shortening

1 egg

1 teaspoon vanilla

¾ teaspoon baking soda

¾ teaspoon ground cinnamon

¼ teaspoon baking powder

¼ teaspoon salt

¼ teaspoon ground nutmeg

½ cup toasted chopped walnuts

½ cup raisins (optional)

Powdered sugar

Makes 9 servings

1. Preheat oven to 350°F. Spray 9-inch square baking pan with nonstick cooking spray.

2. Beat flour, applesauce, brown sugar, shortening, egg, vanilla, baking soda, cinnamon, baking powder, salt and nutmeg in large bowl with stand mixer at low speed 30 seconds. Beat at high speed 3 minutes. Stir in walnuts and raisins, if desired. Pour batter into prepared pan.

3. Bake 30 minutes or until toothpick inserted into center comes out clean. Cool completely in pan on wire rack. Sprinkle with powdered sugar just before serving.

HARVEST QUICK BREAD

1 cup all-purpose flour
1 cup whole wheat flour
½ cup packed brown sugar
¼ cup granulated sugar
1½ teaspoons baking powder
½ teaspoon baking soda
½ teaspoon salt
½ teaspoon ground cinnamon
1 egg
1 cup milk
¼ cup (½ stick) butter, melted
¾ cup dried cranberries
½ cup chopped walnuts

Makes 1 loaf

1. Preheat oven to 350°F. Spray 9×5-inch nonstick loaf pan with nonstick cooking spray.

2. Combine all-purpose flour, whole wheat flour, brown sugar, granulated sugar, baking powder, baking soda, salt and cinnamon in medium bowl. Whisk egg in large bowl. Whisk in milk and butter until blended.

3. Gradually add flour mixture to milk mixture; stir just until moistened. Stir in cranberries and walnuts. Pour batter into prepared pan.

4. Bake 45 to 50 minutes or until toothpick inserted into center comes out clean. Cool in pan on wire rack 10 minutes; remove to wire rack to cool completely.

CHOCOLATE POPOVERS

¾ **cup plus 2 tablespoons all-purpose flour**

¼ **cup granulated sugar**

2 **tablespoons unsweetened cocoa powder**

¼ **teaspoon salt**

4 **eggs**

1 **cup milk**

2 **tablespoons butter, melted**

½ **teaspoon vanilla**

Powdered sugar

Makes 6 popovers

1. Position rack in lower third of oven. Preheat oven to 375°F. Spray 6-cup popover pan or six 6-ounce custard cups with nonstick cooking spray. Set custard cups in jelly-roll pan for easier handling.

2. Sift flour, granulated sugar, cocoa and salt into medium bowl. Beat eggs in large bowl with stand mixer at low speed 1 minute. Add milk, butter and vanilla; beat until blended. Add flour mixture; beat until smooth. Pour batter into prepared pan.

3. Bake 50 minutes. Loosen edges of popovers with knife. Place waxed paper under wire rack. Remove popovers to wire rack; generously sprinkle with powdered sugar. Serve immediately.

Tips: Make sure your popover pan or custard cups are generously greased or else the popovers will stick. For the best results, bring the milk and eggs to room temperature before mixing the batter, and don't fill the individual cups more than half full.

ZUCCHINI BRUNCH BREAD

Bread

- 1 **cup chopped pitted dates**
- 1 **cup water**
- 1 **cup all-purpose flour**
- 1 **cup whole wheat flour**
- 2 **tablespoons granulated sugar**
- 1 **teaspoon baking powder**
- ½ **teaspoon baking soda**
- ½ **teaspoon salt**
- ½ **teaspoon ground cinnamon**
- ¼ **teaspoon ground cloves**
- 2 **eggs**
- 1 **cup shredded zucchini, pressed dry with paper towels**

Cream Cheese Spread (optional)

- 1 **package (8 ounces) cream cheese, softened**
- ¼ **cup powdered sugar**
- 1 **tablespoon vanilla**
- ⅛ **teaspoon ground cinnamon**
  Dash ground cloves

Makes 1 loaf and 1 cup spread

1. Preheat oven to 350°F. Spray 8×4-inch loaf pan with nonstick cooking spray.

2. Combine dates and water in small saucepan; bring to a boil over medium-high heat. Remove from heat; let stand 15 minutes.

3. Combine all-purpose flour, whole wheat flour, granulated sugar, baking powder, baking soda, salt, ½ teaspoon cinnamon and ¼ teaspoon cloves in large bowl. Beat eggs in medium bowl; stir in date mixture and zucchini. Add to flour mixture; stir just until moistened. Pour batter into prepared pan.

4. Bake 30 to 35 minutes or until toothpick inserted into center comes out clean. Cool in pan on wire rack 5 minutes; remove to wire rack to cool completely.

5. Meanwhile, prepare cream cheese spread, if desired. Beat cream cheese, powdered sugar, vanilla, ⅛ teaspoon cinnamon and dash cloves in medium bowl until smooth and well blended. Cover and refrigerate until ready to use. Serve with bread.

PEANUT BUTTER CHOCOLATE CHIP LOAVES

3 **cups all-purpose flour**

1½ **teaspoons baking powder**

1 **teaspoon baking soda**

1 **teaspoon salt**

1 **cup creamy peanut butter**

½ **cup granulated sugar**

½ **cup packed brown sugar**

½ **cup (1 stick) butter, softened**

2 **eggs**

1½ **cups buttermilk***

2 **teaspoons vanilla**

1 **cup mini semisweet chocolate chips**

*Or substitute soured fresh milk. To sour milk, combine 4½ teaspoons lemon juice plus enough milk to equal 1½ cups. Stir; let stand 5 minutes before using.

Makes 2 loaves

1. Preheat oven to 350°F. Spray two 8×4-inch loaf pans with nonstick cooking spray.

2. Sift flour, baking powder, baking soda and salt into medium bowl.

3. Beat peanut butter, granulated sugar, brown sugar and butter in large bowl with stand mixer at medium speed until light and fluffy. Beat in eggs, one at a time, until blended. Beat in buttermilk and vanilla. Gradually add flour mixture; beat at low speed until blended. Stir in chocolate chips. Pour batter into prepared pans.

4. Bake 45 minutes or until toothpick inserted into centers comes out clean. Cool in pans on wire racks 10 minutes; remove to wire racks to cool completely.

Variation: Stir in ¾ cup chocolate chips before baking; sprinkle with remaining ¼ cup chocolate chips after baking.

BANANA BRAN BREAD

1 cup whole bran cereal

½ cup boiling water

1⅓ cups all-purpose flour

1 teaspoon baking powder

½ teaspoon baking soda

¼ teaspoon salt

¼ teaspoon ground cinnamon

½ cup sugar

2 eggs, beaten

2 tablespoons vegetable oil

1 cup ripe mashed bananas (about 2 medium)

¼ cup crumbled unsweetened banana chips

Makes 1 loaf

1. Preheat oven to 350°F. Spray 8×4-inch loaf pan with nonstick cooking spray.

2. Combine cereal and boiling water in small bowl; let stand 10 minutes.

3. Combine flour, baking powder, baking soda, salt and cinnamon in medium bowl. Combine sugar, eggs and oil in large bowl; mix well. Stir in flour mixture and cereal mixture until blended. Stir in mashed bananas. Pour batter into prepared pan; sprinkle with banana chips.

4. Bake 45 to 50 minutes or until toothpick inserted into center comes out clean. Cool in pan on wire rack 5 minutes; remove to wire rack to cool completely.

Variation: Fold in ½ cup dried fruit or sprinkle top of loaf with chopped walnuts or pecans before baking.

DATE NUT BREAD

2 cups all-purpose flour

½ cup packed brown sugar

1 tablespoon baking powder

½ teaspoon salt

¼ cup cold (½ stick) butter, cut into small pieces

1 cup chopped walnuts, toasted*

1 cup chopped dried dates

1¼ cups milk

1 egg

½ teaspoon grated lemon peel

*To toast walnuts, spread in single layer on baking sheet. Toast in preheated 350°F oven 6 to 8 minutes or until browned, stirring frequently.

Makes 1 loaf

1. Preheat oven to 375°F. Spray 9×5-inch loaf pan with nonstick cooking spray.

2. Combine flour, brown sugar, baking powder and salt in large bowl. Cut in butter with pastry blender or two knives until mixture resembles fine crumbs. Stir in walnuts and dates until coated.

3. Beat milk, egg and lemon peel in small bowl until blended. Add to flour mixture; stir just until moistened. Pour batter into prepared pan.

4. Bake 45 to 50 minutes or until toothpick inserted into center comes out clean. Cool in pan on wire rack 10 minutes; remove to wire rack to cool completely.

Tip: To make chopping dates easier, spray your knife with nonstick cooking spray before chopping so the dates won't stick to the knife. (Or purchase chopped dates, which are usually available in the baking or dried fruit section of the supermarket.) One 8-ounce package of pitted dates yields about 1½ cups chopped dates.

ESPRESSO CHOCOLATE MARBLE BREAD

4 cups all-purpose flour

2 teaspoons baking powder

1 teaspoon baking soda

½ teaspoon salt

1½ cups (3 sticks) butter, softened

2 cups sugar

4 eggs

1 tablespoon vanilla

2 cups sour cream

1 tablespoon plus ½ teaspoon instant espresso powder or instant coffee granules, divided

5 tablespoons hot water, divided

¼ cup unsweetened cocoa powder

½ cup semisweet chocolate chips

¼ cup whipping cream

Makes 3 loaves

1. Preheat oven to 350°F. Spray three 8×4-inch loaf pans with nonstick cooking spray.

2. Combine flour, baking powder, baking soda and salt in medium bowl. Beat butter in large bowl with stand mixer until light and creamy. Add sugar; beat 2 minutes. Beat in eggs and vanilla until blended. Add half of flour mixture; beat until blended. Add sour cream; beat about 1 minute or until well blended. Beat in remaining flour mixture.

3. Remove half of batter to medium bowl. Stir 1 tablespoon espresso powder into 2 tablespoons hot water in small bowl until smooth; add to one bowl of batter and mix well. Whisk cocoa and remaining 3 tablespoons water in small bowl until smooth; stir into remaining bowl of batter until well blended. Drop large spoonfuls of batter from each bowl alternately into prepared pans. Swirl batter once or twice with skewer or tip of knife.

4. Bake 45 to 50 minutes or until toothpick inserted into centers comes out clean. Cool in pans on wire racks 10 minutes; remove to wire racks to cool completely.

5. Combine chocolate chips, cream and remaining ½ teaspoon espresso powder in medium microwavable bowl. Microwave on HIGH 20 seconds; stir until smooth. (If necessary, microwave at additional 15-second intervals until chocolate melts.) Drizzle glaze over loaves.

Tip: Disposable foil pans are a great solution if you do not have three loaf pans. Three 9×5-inch pans can be used instead of 8×4-inch pans; loaves will be slightly shorter.

ORANGE WALNUT BREAD

1¾ cups all-purpose flour

½ cup plus 1 tablespoon sugar, divided

1 tablespoon grated orange peel

1½ teaspoons baking powder

¼ teaspoon baking soda

¼ teaspoon salt

¾ cup buttermilk

⅓ cup plus 2 tablespoons orange juice, divided

¼ cup vegetable oil

1 egg

½ cup chopped walnuts

1. Preheat oven to 350°F. Spray 8×4-inch loaf pan with nonstick cooking spray.

2. Combine flour, ½ cup sugar, orange peel, baking powder, baking soda and salt in medium bowl.

3. Whisk buttermilk, ⅓ cup orange juice, oil and egg in small bowl until well blended. Add to flour mixture; stir just until moistened. Fold in walnuts. Pour batter into prepared pan.

4. Bake 50 to 55 minutes or until toothpick inserted into center comes out clean.

5. Whisk remaining 2 tablespoons orange juice and 1 tablespoon sugar in small bowl until sugar is dissolved. Brush over warm bread. Cool in pan on wire rack 10 minutes; remove to wire rack. Serve warm or cool completely.

Makes 1 loaf

SAVORY QUICK BREADS

BROWN SODA BREAD

2 cups all-purpose flour

1 cup whole wheat flour

1 teaspoon baking soda

½ teaspoon salt

½ teaspoon ground ginger

1¼ cups buttermilk, plus additional as needed

3 tablespoons dark molasses

Makes 1 loaf

1. Preheat oven to 375°F. Line baking sheet with parchment paper.

2. Combine all-purpose flour, whole wheat flour, baking soda, salt and ginger in large bowl; mix well. Combine 1½ cups buttermilk and molasses in small bowl; mix well.

3. Stir buttermilk mixture into flour mixture. Add additional buttermilk by tablespoonfuls if necessary to make rough, dry dough. Turn out dough onto floured surface; knead 8 to 10 times or just until smooth. (Do not overknead.) Shape dough into round loaf about 1½ inches thick. Place on prepared baking sheet. Use floured knife to score dough into quarters. Sprinkle top of dough with additional flour, if desired.

4. Bake about 35 minutes or until bread sounds hollow when tapped. Remove to wire rack to cool slightly. Serve warm.

Variations: For a taller loaf, pat dough into round about 2 inches thick. For a seeded topping, omit additional flour on top of dough. Brush with 2 teaspoons buttermilk; press 2 to 3 tablepoons sunflower seeds into dough. Bake as directed above.

BACON-JALAPEÑO CORN BREAD

4 slices bacon

¼ cup minced green onions

2 jalapeño peppers,* seeded and minced

1 cup all-purpose flour

1 cup yellow cornmeal

2½ teaspoons baking powder

¾ teaspoon salt

½ teaspoon baking soda

1 egg

¾ cup plain yogurt

¾ cup milk

¼ cup butter (½ stick), melted

½ cup (2 ounces) shredded Cheddar cheese

*Jalapeño peppers can sting and irritate the skin, so wear rubber gloves when handling peppers and do not touch your eyes.

Makes 9 to 12 servings

1. Preheat oven to 400°F.

2. Cook bacon in large skillet over medium heat until crisp. Drain on paper towel-lined plate. Pour 2 tablespoons drippings into 9-inch square baking pan or cast iron skillet.

3. Crumble bacon into small bowl; add green onions and jalapeños. Combine flour, cornmeal, baking powder, salt and baking soda in large bowl.

4. Whisk egg and yogurt in medium bowl until smooth. Whisk in milk and butter. Add to flour mixture; stir just until moistened. Stir in bacon mixture. Pour into prepared pan; sprinkle with Cheddar.

5. Bake 20 to 25 minutes or until toothpick inserted into center comes out clean. Cool in pan on wire rack 5 minutes. Serve warm.

SOPAIPILLAS

2 cups all-purpose flour

2 teaspoons sugar

2 teaspoons baking powder

½ teaspoon salt

2 tablespoons shortening

¾ cup warm water

Vegetable oil for frying

Makes 16 sopaipillas

1. Combine flour, sugar, baking powder and salt in large bowl. Cut in shortening with pastry blender or two knives until mixture resembles fine crumbs.

2. Gradually add warm water; stir with fork until rough dough forms. Turn out dough onto lightly floured surface; knead 2 minutes or until smooth. Shape dough into a ball; cover and let rest 30 minutes.

3. Divide dough into four pieces; shape each piece into a ball. Flatten each ball into 8-inch circle about ⅛ inch thick. Cut each circle into four wedges.

4. Pour oil into deep heavy skillet to depth of 1½ inches. Heat to 360°F. Cook dough, two pieces at a time, 2 minutes or until puffed and golden brown, turning once. Remove from oil with slotted spoon; drain on paper towels. Serve warm.

Serving Suggestions: In New Mexico, sopaipillas are served in place of bread or filled with ingredients typically used to fill tacos or enchiladas. In other parts of the Southwest and in Mexico, sopaipillas are sprinkled with cinnamon-sugar immediately after frying and served warm with honey.

BOSTON BLACK COFFEE BREAD

½ **cup rye flour**

½ **cup cornmeal**

½ **cup whole wheat flour**

1 **teaspoon baking soda**

½ **teaspoon salt**

¾ **cup strong brewed coffee,**
   room temperature or cold

⅓ **cup molasses**

¼ **cup canola oil**

¾ **cup raisins**

Makes 1 loaf

1. Preheat oven to 325°F. Grease and flour 9×5-inch loaf pan.

2. Combine rye flour, cornmeal, whole wheat flour, baking soda and salt in large bowl. Stir in coffee, molasses and oil until blended. Fold in raisins. Pour batter into prepared pan.

3. Bake 50 minutes or until toothpick inserted into center comes out clean. Cool completely in pan on wire rack.

Tip: To cool hot coffee quickly, pour over 2 ice cubes in a measuring cup to measure ¾ cup total. Let stand 10 minutes to cool.

BRAZILIAN CHEESE ROLLS (PÃO DE QUEIJO)

1 **cup whole milk**

¼ **cup (½ stick) butter, softened**

¼ **cup vegetable oil**

2 **cups plus 2 tablespoons tapioca flour***

2 **eggs**

1 **cup grated Parmesan cheese or other firm cheese**

Sometimes labeled tapioca starch.

Makes about 20 rolls

1. Preheat oven to 350°F.

2. Combine milk, butter and oil in large saucepan; bring to a boil over medium heat, stirring to melt butter. Once mixture reaches a boil, remove from heat. Stir in tapioca flour. Mixture will be thick and stretchy.

3. Stir in eggs, one at a time, and Parmesan. Mixture will be very stiff. Cool in pan until easy to handle.

4. Scoop heaping tablespoonfuls of dough with floured hands and roll into 1½-inch balls. Place about 1 inch apart on ungreased baking sheet.

5. Bake 20 to 25 minutes or until puffed and golden. Serve warm.

Note: These moist, chewy rolls are a Brazilian specialty and are always made with tapioca flour instead of wheat flour. In Brazil they are popular at breakfast, lunch or dinner.

WHEAT GERM BREAD

¾ **cup wheat germ, divided**

¾ **cup all-purpose flour**

½ **cup whole wheat flour**

¼ **cup packed brown sugar**

1 **teaspoon baking soda**

½ **teaspoon baking powder**

¼ **teaspoon salt**

½ **cup raisins**

1 **cup buttermilk***

¼ **cup (½ stick) butter, melted**

1 **egg**

Or substitute soured fresh milk. To sour milk, combine 1 tablespoon lemon juice plus enough milk to equal 1 cup. Stir; let stand 5 minutes.

Makes 1 loaf

1. Preheat oven to 350°F. Spray 8×4-inch loaf pan with nonstick cooking spray. Reserve 2 tablespoons wheat germ for topping.

2. Combine remaining wheat germ, all-purpose flour, whole wheat flour, brown sugar, baking soda, baking powder and salt in large bowl. Add raisins; stir until coated.

3. Whisk buttermilk, butter and egg in small bowl until blended. Add to flour mixture; stir just until moistened. Pour batter into prepared pan; sprinkle with reserved 2 tablespoons wheat germ.

4. Bake 40 to 50 minutes or until toothpick inserted into center comes out clean. Cool in pan on wire rack 10 minutes; remove to wire rack. Serve warm or cool completely.

CHEDDAR-BEER HUSH PUPPIES

Vegetable oil for frying

1½ **cups medium grain cornmeal**

1 **cup all-purpose flour**

2 **tablespoons sugar**

1 **teaspoon baking powder**

1 **teaspoon baking soda**

1 **teaspoon salt**

¼ **teaspoon black pepper**

1 **bottle (12 ounces) lager or other light-colored beer**

1 **egg, beaten**

¾ **cup (3 ounces) shredded Cheddar cheese**

2 **jalapeño peppers,* seeded and minced**

*Jalapeño peppers can sting and irritate the skin, so wear rubber gloves when handling peppers and do not touch your eyes.

Makes about 36 hush puppies

1. Pour oil into large saucepan to depth of 3 inches; heat over medium heat to 350°F. Line baking sheet with three layers of paper towels.

2. Combine cornmeal, flour, sugar, baking powder, baking soda, salt and black pepper in large bowl. Whisk beer and egg in medium bowl until blended. Gradually whisk into cornmeal mixture until smooth. Stir in Cheddar and jalapeños.

3. Working in batches, drop heaping tablespoonfuls of batter into hot oil. Cook 2 minutes or until golden brown, turning occasionally. Transfer to prepared baking sheet to drain. Serve immediately.

FIESTA BREAD

½ **pound chorizo sausage, casings removed**

½ **cup chopped onion**

1¼ **cups all-purpose flour**

1 **cup cornmeal**

1½ **teaspoons baking soda**

1 **teaspoon ground cumin**

½ **teaspoon salt**

1 **cup Mexican beer**

1 **cup (4 ounces) shredded Cheddar cheese**

1 **can (4 ounces) diced green chiles, drained**

1 **egg, beaten**

Makes 8 servings

1. Preheat oven to 375°F. Spray 8-inch square baking pan with nonstick cooking spray.

2. Brown sausage and onion in medium skillet over medium-high heat, stirring to break up meat. Drain fat.

3. Combine flour, cornmeal, baking soda, cumin and salt in large bowl. Combine beer, Cheddar, chiles and egg in medium bowl; mix well. Add to flour mixture; stir just until moistened. Stir in sausage mixture. Pour batter into prepared pan.

4. Bake 20 minutes or until toothpick inserted into center comes out clean. Cool in pan on wire rack 10 minutes. Serve warm. Refrigerate leftovers.

IRISH SODA BREAD

2½ cups all-purpose flour

1¼ cups whole wheat flour

1 cup currants

¼ cup sugar

4 teaspoons baking powder

2 teaspoons caraway seeds (optional)

1 teaspoon salt

½ teaspoon baking soda

½ cup (1 stick) butter, cut into small pieces

1⅓ to 1½ cups buttermilk

Makes 1 loaf

1. Preheat oven to 350°F. Line baking sheet with parchment paper.

2. Combine all-purpose flour, whole wheat flour, currants, sugar, baking powder, caraway seeds, if desired, salt and baking soda in large bowl.

3. Cut in butter with pastry blender or two knives until mixture resembles coarse crumbs. Add buttermilk; mix until slightly sticky dough forms. Transfer dough to prepared baking sheet; shape into 8-inch round.

4. Bake 50 to 60 minutes or until golden brown and crust is firm. Cool on baking sheet 10 minutes; remove to wire rack to cool completely.

AREPAS (LATIN AMERICAN CORN CAKES)

1½ **cups instant corn flour for arepas***

½ **teaspoon salt**

1½ **to 2 cups hot water**

⅓ **cup shredded Mexican cheese blend**

1 **tablespoon butter, melted**

*This flour is also called masarepa, masa al instante and harina precodica. It is not the same as masa harina or regular cornmeal. Purchase arepa flour at Latin American markets or online.

Makes 6 to 8 arepas

1. Preheat oven to 350°F. Combine instant corn flour and salt in medium bowl. Stir in 1½ cups hot water until dough forms. Dough should be smooth and moist but not sticky; add additional water, 1 tablespoon at a time, if necessary. Add cheese and butter; knead until dough is consistency of smooth mashed potatoes.

2. Lightly grease heavy skillet or griddle; heat over medium heat. Divide dough into six to eight pieces; flatten and pat dough into 4-inch discs about ½ inch thick. (If dough cracks or is too dry, return to bowl and add additional water, 1 tablespoon at a time.)

3. Immediately place dough pieces in hot skillet. Cook 3 to 5 minutes per side or until browned in spots. Remove to ungreased baking sheet.

4. Bake 15 minutes or until arepas sound hollow when tapped. Serve warm.

Arepa Breakfast Sandwiches: Split arepas by piercing edges with fork as you would English muffins. Fill with scrambled eggs, cheese and salsa.

Tip: Freeze leftover arepas in airtight freezer food storage bags.

FRUIT-FILLED MUFFINS

STRAWBERRY MUFFINS

1¼ cups all-purpose flour

2½ teaspoons baking powder

½ teaspoon salt

1 cup old-fashioned oats

½ cup sugar

1 cup milk

½ cup (1 stick) butter, melted

1 egg, beaten

1 teaspoon vanilla

1 cup chopped fresh
    strawberries

Makes 12 muffins

1. Preheat oven to 425°F. Line 12 standard (2½-inch) muffin cups with paper baking cups or spray with nonstick cooking spray.

2. Combine flour, baking powder and salt in large bowl. Stir in oats and sugar.

3. Whisk milk, butter, egg and vanilla in medium bowl until well blended. Add to flour mixture; stir just until moistened. Fold in strawberries. Spoon evenly into prepared muffin cups.

4. Bake 15 to 18 minutes or until lightly browned and toothpick inserted into centers comes out clean. Cool in pan on wire rack 5 minutes; remove to wire rack. Serve warm or cool completely.

HONEY FIG WHOLE WHEAT MUFFINS

 1 cup whole wheat flour

½ cup all-purpose flour

½ cup wheat germ

 2 teaspoons baking powder

 1 teaspoon ground cinnamon

½ teaspoon salt

½ teaspoon ground nutmeg

½ cup milk

½ cup honey

¼ cup (½ stick) butter, melted

 1 egg

 1 cup chopped dried figs

½ cup chopped walnuts

Makes 12 muffins

1. Preheat oven to 375°F. Line 12 standard (2½-inch) muffin cups with paper baking cups or spray with nonstick cooking spray.

2. Combine whole wheat flour, all-purpose flour, wheat germ, baking powder, cinnamon, salt and nutmeg in large bowl.

3. Whisk milk, honey, butter and egg in small bowl until well blended. Add to flour mixture; stir just until moistened. Fold in figs and walnuts. Spoon evenly into prepared muffin cups.

4. Bake 20 minutes or until edges are lightly browned and toothpick inserted into centers comes out clean. Cool in pan on wire rack 5 minutes; remove to wire rack. Serve warm or cool completely.

PECAN PEACH MUFFINS

**Pecan Topping
(recipe follows)**

1½ **cups all-purpose flour**

½ **cup granulated sugar**

2 **teaspoons baking powder**

1 **teaspoon ground cinnamon**

¼ **teaspoon salt**

½ **cup (1 stick) butter, melted**

¼ **cup milk**

1 **egg**

2 **peaches, peeled and diced
(about 1 cup)**

Makes 12 muffins

1. Preheat oven to 400°F. Line 12 standard (2½-inch) muffin cups with paper baking cups or spray with nonstick cooking spray. Prepare Pecan Topping.

2. Combine flour, granulated sugar, baking powder, cinnamon and salt in large bowl.

3. Whisk butter, milk and egg in small bowl until blended. Add to flour mixture; stir just until moistened. Gently fold in peaches. Spoon batter evenly into prepared muffin cups; sprinkle with Pecan Topping.

4. Bake 20 to 25 minutes or until toothpick inserted into centers come out clean. Cool in pan on wire rack 5 minutes; remove to wire rack. Serve warm or cool completely.

Pecan Topping: Combine ½ cup chopped pecans, ⅓ cup packed brown sugar, ¼ cup all-purpose flour and 1 teaspoon ground cinnamon in small bowl. Add 2 tablespoons melted butter; stir until crumbly.

BANANA PEANUT BUTTER CHIP MUFFINS

2 cups all-purpose flour

¾ cup sugar

2 teaspoons baking powder

½ teaspoon baking soda

¼ teaspoon salt

1 cup mashed ripe bananas (about 2 large)

½ cup (1 stick) butter, melted

2 eggs, beaten

⅓ cup buttermilk

1½ teaspoons vanilla

1 cup peanut butter chips

½ cup chopped peanuts

Makes 15 muffins

1. Preheat oven to 375°F. Line 15 standard (2½-inch) muffins cups with paper baking cups or spray with nonstick cooking spray.

2. Combine flour, sugar, baking powder, baking soda and salt in large bowl.

3. Beat bananas, butter, eggs, buttermilk and vanilla in medium bowl until well blended. Add to flour mixture; stir just until moistened. Gently fold in peanut butter chips. Spoon batter evenly into prepared muffin cups; sprinkle with chopped peanuts.

4. Bake 20 minutes or until toothpick inserted into centers comes out clean. Cool in pans on wire racks 5 minutes; remove to wire racks. Serve warm or cool completely.

Tip: Substitute a mixture of chocolate and peanut butter chips for the peanut butter chips for a combination of three great flavors in one muffin.

CRANBERRY-OATMEAL MINI MUFFINS

1 cup quick oats

¾ cup milk

1 egg, beaten

3 tablespoons butter, melted

1 cup all-purpose flour

⅓ cup packed brown sugar

1 tablespoon baking powder

½ teaspoon baking soda

½ teaspoon ground cinnamon

¼ teaspoon salt

½ cup finely chopped dried cranberries

Makes 24 muffins

1. Preheat oven to 375°F. Spray 24 mini (1¾-inch) muffin cups with nonstick cooking spray.

2. Combine oats and milk in large bowl; let stand 5 minutes to soften. Stir in egg and butter until blended.

3. Combine flour, brown sugar, baking powder, baking soda, cinnamon and salt in small bowl. Add to oat mixture; stir just until dry ingredients are moistened. Fold in cranberries. Spoon batter evenly into prepared muffin cups.

4. Bake 12 to 15 minutes or until toothpick inserted into centers comes out clean. Cool in pans on wire racks 1 minute; remove to wire racks. Serve warm or cool completely.

GINGERBREAD PEAR MUFFINS

1¾ cups all-purpose flour

⅓ cup sugar

2 teaspoons baking powder

¾ teaspoon ground ginger

¼ teaspoon baking soda

¼ teaspoon salt

¼ teaspoon ground cinnamon

⅓ cup milk

¼ cup vegetable oil

¼ cup light molasses

1 egg

1 medium pear, peeled and finely chopped

Makes 12 muffins

1. Preheat oven to 375°F. Line 12 standard (2½-inch) muffin cups with paper baking cups or spray with nonstick cooking spray.

2. Sift flour, sugar, baking powder, ginger, baking soda, salt and cinnamon into large bowl.

3. Whisk milk, oil, molasses and egg in medium bowl. Stir in pear. Add to flour mixture; stir just until moistened. Spoon batter evenly into prepared muffin cups.

4. Bake 20 minutes or until toothpick inserted into centers comes out clean. Cool in pan on wire rack 5 minutes; remove to wire rack. Serve warm or cool completely.

BERRY BRAN MUFFINS

2 cups whole bran cereal

1¼ cups milk

½ cup packed brown sugar

¼ cup vegetable oil

1 egg

1 teaspoon vanilla

1¼ cups all-purpose flour

1 tablespoon baking powder

¼ teaspoon salt

1 cup fresh or frozen blueberries (partially thawed if frozen)

Makes 12 muffins

1. Preheat oven to 350°F. Line 12 standard (2¾-inch) muffin cups with paper baking cups or spray with nonstick cooking spray.

2. Combine cereal and milk in medium bowl; let stand 5 minutes to soften. Stir in brown sugar, oil, egg and vanilla until blended.

3. Combine flour, baking powder and salt in large bowl. Add cereal mixture; stir just until moistened. Gently fold in berries. Spoon batter evenly into prepared muffin cups.

4. Bake 20 to 25 minutes (25 to 30 minutes if using frozen berries) or until toothpick inserted into centers comes out clean. Cool in pan on wire rack 5 minutes; remove to wire rack. Serve warm or cool completely.

JUMBO STREUSEL-TOPPED RASPBERRY MUFFINS

2¼ cups all-purpose flour, divided

¼ cup packed brown sugar

2 tablespoons cold butter

¾ cup granulated sugar

2 teaspoons baking powder

½ teaspoon baking soda

½ teaspoon salt

½ teaspoon grated lemon peel

¾ cup plus 2 tablespoons milk

⅓ cup butter, melted

1 egg, beaten

2 cups fresh or frozen raspberries (do not thaw)

Makes 6 jumbo muffins

1. Preheat oven to 350°F. Spray 6 jumbo (3½-inch) muffin cups with nonstick cooking spray.

2. For topping, combine ¼ cup flour and brown sugar in small bowl. Cut in cold butter with pastry blender or two knives until mixture forms coarse crumbs.

3. Reserve ¼ cup flour in medium bowl. Combine remaining 1¾ cups flour, granulated sugar, baking powder, baking soda, salt and lemon peel in medium bowl.

4. Whisk milk, melted butter and egg in small bowl until blended. Add to flour mixture; stir just until moistened. Toss raspberries with reserved flour in small bowl; gently fold into batter. Spoon batter evenly into prepared muffin cups. Sprinkle with topping.

5. Bake 25 to 30 minutes or until toothpick inserted into centers comes out clean. Cool in pan on wire rack 5 minutes; remove to wire rack. Serve warm or cool completely.

Variation: For smaller muffins, spoon batter into 12 standard (2½-inch) greased or paper-lined muffin cups. Bake 21 to 24 minutes or until toothpick inserted into centers comes out clean.

APPLE BUTTER SPICE MUFFINS

½ **cup sugar**

1 **teaspoon ground cinnamon**

¼ **teaspoon ground nutmeg**

⅛ **teaspoon ground allspice**

½ **cup chopped pecans or walnuts**

2 **cups all-purpose flour**

2 **teaspoons baking powder**

¼ **teaspoon salt**

1 **cup milk**

¼ **cup vegetable oil**

1 **egg**

¼ **cup apple butter**

Makes 12 muffins

1. Preheat oven to 400°F. Line 12 standard (2½-inch) muffin cups with paper baking cups or spray with nonstick cooking spray.

2. Combine sugar, cinnamon, nutmeg and allspice in large bowl. Combine 2 tablespoons sugar mixture and pecans in small bowl; mix well. Add flour, baking powder and salt to remaining sugar mixture.

3. Whisk milk, oil and egg in medium bowl until blended. Add to flour mixture; stir just until moistened.

4. Spoon 1 tablespoon batter into each prepared muffin cup; top with 1 teaspoon apple butter. Spoon remaining batter evenly over apple butter. Sprinkle with pecan mixture.

5. Bake 20 to 25 minutes or until golden brown and toothpick inserted into centers comes out clean. Cool in pan on wire rack 10 minutes; remove to wire rack. Serve warm or cool completely.

APRICOT MINI MUFFINS

1½ **cups all-purpose flour**

½ **cup sugar**

½ **cup finely chopped dried apricots**

¼ **teaspoon baking powder**

¼ **teaspoon baking soda**

⅛ **teaspoon salt**

Pinch ground nutmeg

½ **cup (1 stick) butter, melted and cooled**

2 **eggs**

2 **tablespoons milk**

1 **teaspoon vanilla**

Makes 24 mini muffins

1. Preheat oven to 350°F. Spray 24 mini (1¾-inch) muffin cups with nonstick cooking spray.

2. Combine flour, sugar, apricots, baking powder, baking soda, salt and nutmeg in large bowl.

3. Whisk butter, eggs, milk and vanilla in medium bowl until blended. Add to flour mixture; stir just until moistened. Spoon batter evenly into prepared muffin cups.

4. Bake 12 to 15 minutes or until toothpick inserted into centers comes out clean. Cool in pans on wire racks 5 minutes; remove to wire racks. Serve warm or cool completely.

Tip: Muffin batter should only be stirred until all the dry ingredients are moistened—don't worry if there are lumps. If the batter is overbeaten, the resulting muffins will be tough.

ANYTIME MUFFINS

CARROT OAT MUFFINS

¾ **cup all-purpose flour**

¾ **cup whole wheat flour**

¾ **cup old-fashioned oats**

½ **cup sugar**

1½ **teaspoons baking powder**

¾ **teaspoon ground cinnamon**

½ **teaspoon baking soda**

½ **teaspoon salt**

½ **cup milk**

½ **cup unsweetened applesauce**

2 **eggs**

¼ **cup canola oil**

½ **cup shredded carrot**

¼ **cup finely chopped walnuts (optional)**

Makes 12 muffins

1. Preheat oven to 350°F. Spray 12 standard (2½-inch) muffin cups with nonstick cooking spray.

2. Combine all-purpose flour, whole wheat flour, oats, sugar, baking powder, cinnamon, baking soda and salt in medium bowl.

3. Whisk milk, applesauce, eggs and oil in large bowl until blended. Stir in carrot. Add flour mixture to applesauce mixture; stir just until moistened. (Do not overmix.) Spoon batter evenly into prepared muffin cups. Sprinkle with walnuts, if desired.

4. Bake 20 to 22 minutes or until golden brown and toothpick inserted into centers comes out clean. Cool in pan on wire rack 5 minutes; remove to wire rack. Serve warm or cool completely.

Note: These muffins are best eaten the same day they are baked.

PUMPKIN CHOCOLATE CHIP MUFFINS

2½ cups all-purpose flour

1 tablespoon baking powder

1½ teaspoons pumpkin pie spice*

½ teaspoon salt

1 cup packed brown sugar

1 cup solid-pack pumpkin

¾ cup milk

6 tablespoons (¾ stick) butter, melted

2 eggs

1 cup semisweet chocolate chips

½ cup chopped walnuts

*Or substitute ¾ teaspoon ground cinnamon, ½ teaspoon ground ginger and ¼ teaspoon each ground allspice and ground nutmeg.

Makes 18 muffins

1. Preheat oven to 400°F. Line 18 standard (2½-inch) muffin cups with paper baking cups or spray with nonstick cooking spray.

2. Combine flour, baking powder, pumpkin pie spice and salt in large bowl.

3. Whisk brown sugar, pumpkin, milk, butter and eggs in medium bowl until well blended. Add pumpkin mixture, chocolate chips and walnuts to flour mixture; stir just until moistened. Spoon evenly into prepared muffin cups.

4. Bake 15 minutes or until toothpick inserted into centers comes out clean. Cool in pans on wire racks 5 minutes; remove to wire racks. Serve warm or cool completely.

JALAPEÑO CORN MUFFINS

1½ cups yellow cornmeal

¾ cup all-purpose flour

2 teaspoons baking powder

½ teaspoon baking soda

½ teaspoon salt

¾ cup buttermilk

2 eggs

¼ cup (½ stick) butter, melted

2 tablespoons sugar

1 can (8 ounces) cream-style corn

1 cup (4 ounces) shredded Monterey Jack or Cheddar cheese

2 jalapeño peppers,* seeded and finely chopped

*Jalapeño peppers can sting and irritate the skin, so wear rubber gloves when handling peppers and do not touch your eyes.

Makes 18 muffins

1. Preheat oven to 400°F. Spray 18 standard (2½-inch) muffin cups with nonstick cooking spray.

2. Combine cornmeal, flour, baking powder, baking soda and salt in large bowl.

3. Whisk buttermilk, eggs, butter and sugar in medium bowl until well blended. Add to flour mixture; stir just until moistened. Add corn, cheese and jalapeños; stir just until blended. Spoon batter evenly into prepared muffin cups.

4. Bake 15 to 17 minutes or until golden brown and toothpick inserted into centers comes out clean. Cool in pans on wire racks 5 minutes; remove to wire racks. Serve warm.

SUN-DRIED TOMATO BASIL MUFFINS

½ cup sun-dried tomatoes
    (not packed in oil)

2 cups all-purpose flour

1 tablespoon baking powder

1½ teaspoons dried basil

½ teaspoon salt

¼ teaspoon black pepper

⅛ teaspoon garlic powder

¾ cup milk

½ cup cottage cheese

1 egg

¼ cup canola oil

2 teaspoons minced dried
    onion

Makes 12 servings

1. Preheat oven to 400°F. Spray 12 standard (2½-inch) muffin cups with nonstick cooking spray. Place sun-dried tomatoes in small bowl; cover with boiling water. Let stand 10 minutes to soften. Drain and finely chop.

2. Combine flour, baking powder, basil, salt, pepper and garlic powder in large bowl.

3. Whisk milk, cottage cheese, egg, oil, onion and sun-dried tomatoes in medium bowl until well blended. Add to flour mixture; stir just until moistened. Spoon batter evenly into prepared muffin cups.

4. Bake 20 to 25 minutes or until toothpick inserted into centers comes out clean. Cool in pan on wire rack 5 minutes; remove to wire rack. Serve warm.

WILD RICE MUFFINS

½ cup all-purpose flour

½ cup whole wheat flour

1½ teaspoons baking powder

1 teaspoon baking soda

¼ teaspoon salt

¼ teaspoon ground cinnamon

⅓ cup packed dark brown sugar

¼ cup (½ stick) butter, softened

1 egg

½ to ⅔ cup milk

1 cup cooked wild rice

½ cup coarsely chopped pecans

½ cup chopped dried dates

Makes 12 muffins

1. Preheat oven to 400°F. Spray 12 standard (2½-inch) muffin cups with nonstick cooking spray.

2. Combine all-purpose flour, whole wheat flour, baking powder, baking soda, salt and cinnamon in medium bowl.

3. Beat brown sugar and butter in large bowl with electric mixer at high speed until creamy. Add egg; beat at medium speed until blended. Add ½ cup milk; beat until blended. Beat in wild rice at low speed. Add flour mixture to batter in two parts; beat at medium speed just until blended. (Do not overmix. Batter should be somewhat wet; if batter is stiff, add remaining milk, 1 tablespoon at a time.) Gently stir in pecans and dates. Spoon batter evenly into prepared muffin cups.

4. Bake 12 to 15 minutes or until toothpick inserted into centers comes out clean. Cool in pan on wire rack 5 minutes; remove to wire rack. Serve warm or cool completely.

LEMON-GLAZED ZUCCHINI MUFFINS

2 cups all-purpose flour

⅔ cup granulated sugar

1 tablespoon baking powder

2 teaspoons grated lemon peel

1 teaspoon salt

½ teaspoon ground nutmeg

½ cup chopped walnuts, pecans or hazelnuts

½ cup dried fruit bits or golden raisins

½ cup milk

2 eggs

⅓ cup vegetable oil

1 cup packed shredded zucchini, undrained

¼ cup powdered sugar

1 to 1½ teaspoons lemon juice

1. Preheat oven to 400°F. Line 12 standard (2½-inch) muffin cups with paper baking cups or spray with nonstick cooking spray.

2. Combine flour, granulated sugar, baking powder, lemon peel, salt and nutmeg in large bowl; stir in walnuts and dried fruit.

3. Whisk milk, eggs and oil in small bowl until well blended. Add to flour mixture with zucchini; stir just until moistened. Spoon batter evenly into prepared muffin cups.

4. Bake 20 to 25 minutes or until toothpick inserted into centers comes out clean. Remove to wire rack to cool slightly.

5. Meanwhile, whisk powdered sugar and lemon juice in small bowl until smooth. Drizzle over warm muffins.

Makes 12 muffins

SWEET POTATO MUFFINS

2 cups all-purpose flour

¾ cup chopped walnuts

¾ cup golden raisins

½ cup packed brown sugar

1 tablespoon baking powder

1 teaspoon ground cinnamon

½ teaspoon salt

½ teaspoon baking soda

¼ teaspoon ground nutmeg

1 cup mashed cooked sweet potato

¾ cup milk

½ cup (1 stick) butter, melted

2 eggs, beaten

1½ teaspoons vanilla

Makes 24 muffins

1. Preheat oven to 400°F. Spray 24 standard (2½-inch) muffin cups with nonstick cooking spray.

2. Combine flour, walnuts, raisins, brown sugar, baking powder, cinnamon, salt, baking soda and nutmeg in medium bowl.

3. Whisk sweet potato, milk, butter, eggs and vanilla in large bowl until well blended. Add flour mixture; stir just until moistened. Spoon batter evenly into prepared muffin cups.

4. Bake 15 minutes or until toothpick inserted into centers comes out clean. Cool in pans on wire racks 5 minutes; remove to wire racks. Serve warm or cool completely.

BACON, ONION AND PARMESAN MUFFINS

6 slices bacon, chopped

2 cups chopped onions

3 teaspoons sugar, divided

¼ teaspoon dried thyme

1½ cups all-purpose flour

¾ cup grated Parmesan cheese

2 teaspoons baking powder

½ teaspoon salt

¾ cup lager or other light-colored beer

2 eggs

¼ cup extra virgin olive oil

Makes 12 muffins

1. Preheat oven to 375°F. Spray 12 standard (2½-inch) muffin cups with nonstick cooking spray.

2. Cook bacon in large skillet over medium heat until crisp, stirring occasionally. Remove to paper towel-lined plate with slotted spoon, leaving drippings in skillet. Add onions, 1 teaspoon sugar and thyme to skillet; cook 12 minutes or until onions are golden brown, stirring occasionally. Cool 5 minutes; stir in bacon.

3. Combine flour, Parmesan, baking powder, salt and remaining 2 teaspoons sugar in large bowl.

4. Whisk lager, eggs and oil in medium bowl until well blended. Add to flour mixture; stir just until moistened. Gently stir in onion mixture. Spoon batter evenly into prepared muffin cups.

5. Bake 15 minutes or until toothpick inserted into centers comes out clean. Cool in pan on wire rack 5 minutes; remove to wire rack. Serve warm or cool completely.

GINGER SQUASH MUFFINS

1½ cups all-purpose flour

⅓ cup whole wheat flour

⅓ cup granulated sugar

¼ cup packed dark brown sugar

2½ teaspoons baking powder

1 teaspoon ground cinnamon

½ teaspoon baking soda

½ teaspoon salt

½ teaspoon ground ginger

1 package (12 ounces) frozen winter squash, thawed*

2 eggs, beaten

⅓ cup canola oil

¼ cup finely chopped walnuts

2 tablespoons finely chopped crystallized ginger (optional)

*Or use puréed cooked fresh butternut squash.

Makes 12 muffins

1. Preheat oven to 375°F. Spray 12 standard (2½-inch) muffin cups with nonstick cooking spray.

2. Combine all-purpose flour, whole wheat flour, granulated sugar, brown sugar, baking powder, cinnamon, baking soda, salt and ground ginger in large bowl.

3. Whisk squash, eggs and oil in medium bowl until well blended. Add to flour mixture; stir just until moistened. Stir in walnuts and crystallized ginger, if desired. Spoon batter evenly into prepared muffin cups.

4. Bake 18 to 20 minutes or until toothpick inserted into centers comes out clean. Cool in pan on wire rack 5 minutes; remove to wire rack. Serve warm or cool completely.

PEANUT BUTTER BRAN MUFFINS

½ **cup peanut butter**

¼ **cup packed brown sugar**

1 **egg**

2 **tablespoons butter, softened**

1 **cup whole bran cereal**

1 **cup milk**

¾ **cup all-purpose flour**

1 **tablespoon baking powder**

½ **teaspoon salt**

½ **cup dark raisins**

Makes 12 muffins

1. Heat oven to 400°F. Spray 12 standard (2½-inch) muffin cups with nonstick cooking spray or line with paper baking cups.

2. Combine peanut butter, brown sugar, egg and butter in food pocessor; process 10 seconds or until smooth. Add cereal and milk; pulse just until blended.

3. Add flour, baking powder and salt; pulse 2 to 3 times or just until flour is moistened. (Do not overprocess. Batter should be lumpy.) Sprinkle raisins over batter; pulse just until raisins are incorporated. Spoon batter evenly into prepared muffin cups.

4. Bake 20 to 25 minutes or until golden brown and toothpick inserted into centers comes out clean. Cool in pan on wire rack 5 minutes; remove to wire rack. Serve warm or cool completely.

SCONES

PUMPKIN-GINGER SCONES

½ cup sugar, divided

2 cups all-purpose flour

2 teaspoons baking powder

1 teaspoon ground cinnamon

½ teaspoon baking soda

½ teaspoon salt

¼ cup (½ stick) cold butter, cut into small pieces

1 egg

½ cup solid-pack pumpkin

¼ cup sour cream

½ teaspoon grated fresh ginger *or* 2 tablespoons finely chopped crystallized ginger

1 tablespoon butter, melted

Makes 12 scones

1. Preheat oven to 425°F.

2. Reserve 1 tablespoon sugar. Combine remaining sugar, flour, baking powder, cinnamon, baking soda and salt in large bowl. Cut in cold butter with pastry blender or two knives until mixture resembles coarse crumbs.

3. Whisk egg in medium bowl. Add pumpkin, sour cream and ginger; whisk until well blended. Add to flour mixture; stir just until soft dough forms.

4. Turn out dough onto well-floured surface; knead 10 times. Roll out dough into 9×6-inch rectangle. with floured rolling pin. Cut into six 3-inch squares with floured knife; cut diagonally into halves to form 12 triangles. Place 2 inches apart on ungreased baking sheets. Brush with melted butter; sprinkle with reserved sugar.

5. Bake 10 to 12 minutes or until golden brown. Remove to wire racks to cool 10 minutes. Serve warm.

ENGLISH-STYLE SCONES

2 cups all-purpose flour

2 teaspoons baking powder

¼ teaspoon salt

¼ cup (½ stick) cold butter, cut into pieces

¼ cup finely chopped pitted dates

¼ cup golden raisins or currants

3 eggs, divided

½ cup whipping cream

1½ teaspoons vanilla

1 teaspoon water

Makes 6 scones

1. Preheat oven to 375°F. Spray baking sheet with nonstick cooking spray or line with parchment paper.

2. Combine flour, baking powder and salt in medium bowl. Cut in butter with pastry blender or two knives until mixture resembles coarse crumbs. Stir in dates and raisins.

3. Whisk 2 eggs, cream and vanilla in medium bowl until well blended. Add to flour mixture; stir just until moistened.

4. Turn out dough onto lightly floured surface; knead 4 times. Place dough on prepared baking sheet; pat into 8-inch circle. Gently score dough into six wedges with sharp wet knife, cutting three-fourths of the way through dough. Beat remaining egg and water in small bowl; brush lightly over dough.

5. Bake 18 to 20 minutes or until golden brown. Remove to wire rack to cool 5 minutes. Serve warm.

COCONUT SCONES WITH ORANGE BUTTER

1¾ cups all-purpose flour

2 tablespoons sugar

1 tablespoon baking powder

½ teaspoon salt

⅓ cup cold butter, cut into small pieces

1 cup whipping cream, divided

½ cup plus ⅓ cup flaked coconut, divided

1 egg, beaten

2 tablespoons milk

2 teaspoons grated orange peel

Orange Butter (recipe follows)

Makes 8 scones

1. Preheat oven to 400°F. Line baking sheet with parchment paper.

2. Combine flour, sugar, baking powder and salt in large bowl. Cut in butter with pastry blender or two knives until mixture resembles coarse crumbs.

3. Whisk ¾ cup cream, ½ cup coconut, egg, milk and orange peel in medium bowl until well blended. Add to flour mixture; stir just until soft dough forms.

4. Turn out dough onto lightly floured surface; pat into 8-inch circle about ¾ inch thick. Cut into eight wedges. Place 2 inches apart on prepared baking sheet. Brush tops of scones with remaining ¼ cup cream; sprinkle with remaining ⅓ cup coconut.

5. Bake 12 to 15 minutes or until golden brown. Remove to wire rack to cool 15 minutes. Prepare Orange Butter; serve with warm scones.

Orange Butter: Combine ½ cup (1 stick) softened butter, 2 tablespoons orange juice, 1 tablespoon grated orange peel and 2 teaspons sugar in large bowl; beat with stand mixer at medium speed until creamy.

CHOCOLATE CHIP SCONES

2 cups all-purpose flour

1 cup mini semisweet
   chocolate chips

¾ cup golden raisins

½ cup sugar

2 teaspoons baking powder

¼ teaspoon baking soda

¼ teaspoon salt

¼ teaspoon ground cinnamon

½ cup (1 stick) cold butter,
   cut into small pieces

½ cup buttermilk

2 eggs, divided

½ teaspoon vanilla

1 tablespoon milk

Makes 24 scones

1. Preheat oven to 350°F. Line baking sheets with parchment paper.

2. Combine flour, chocolate chips, raisins, sugar, baking powder, baking soda, salt and cinnamon in large bowl. Cut in butter with pastry blender or two knives until mixture resembles coarse crumbs.

3. Whisk buttermillk, 1 egg and vanilla in medium bowl until well blended. Add to flour mixture; stir just until sticky dough forms.

4. Drop dough by 2 tablespoonfuls onto prepared baking sheets. Beat remaining egg and milk in small bowl; brush over tops of scones.

5. Bake 12 to 14 minutes or until toothpick inserted into centers comes out clean. Remove to wire rack to cool 5 minutes. Serve warm.

BROCCOLI AND CHEDDAR SCONES

2½ cups all-purpose flour

1 tablespoon baking powder

1 tablespoon sugar

2 teaspoons salt

½ teaspoon red pepper flakes

1 cup broccoli florets

½ cup (1 stick) cold butter, cut into small pieces

1½ cups shredded Cheddar cheese

1 cup milk

Makes 16 scones

1. Preheat oven to 400°F. Line baking sheets with parchment paper.

2. Combine flour, baking powder, sugar, salt and red pepper flakes in food processor; process 10 seconds. Add broccoli and butter; process until mixture forms coarse crumbs, scraping down side of bowl once.

3. Transfer mixture into large bowl. Add Cheddar and milk; stir just until moistened. Lightly knead mixture to form dough.

4. Divide dough in half. Pat one half of dough into 8-inch circle. Cut into eight wedges; place 2 inches apart on prepared baking sheet. Repeat with second half of dough.

5. Bake 15 to 20 minutes or until lightly browned. Remove to wire racks to cool 5 minutes. Serve warm.

OAT AND WHOLE WHEAT SCONES

1 cup old-fashioned oats

1 cup whole wheat flour

½ cup all-purpose flour

¼ cup sugar

1 tablespoon baking powder

¼ teaspoon salt

½ cup (1 stick) cold butter, cut into small pieces

½ cup whipping cream

1 egg

¾ cup dried cherries

Makes 8 scones

1. Preheat oven to 425°F. Line baking sheet with parchment paper.

2. Combine oats, whole wheat flour, all-purpose flour, sugar, baking powder and salt in large bowl. Cut in butter with pastry blender or two knives until mixture resembles coarse crumbs.

3. Whisk cream and egg in small bowl until well blended. Add to flour mixture; stir just until dough comes together. Stir in cherries.

4. Turn out dough onto lightly floured surface; shape into 8-inch circle about ¾ inch thick. Cut into eight wedges; place 2 inches apart on prepared baking sheet.

5. Bake about 15 minutes or until golden brown. Remove to wire rack to cool 5 minutes. Serve warm.

CRANBERRY SCONES

1½ cups all-purpose flour

½ cup oat bran

¼ cup plus 1 tablespoon sugar, divided

2 teaspoons baking powder

½ teaspoon baking soda

½ teaspoon salt

⅓ cup cold butter, cut into small pieces

¾ cup dried cranberries

⅓ cup milk

1 egg

¼ cup sour cream

1 tablespoon old-fashioned or quick oats (optional)

Makes 12 scones

1. Preheat oven to 425°F.

2. Combine flour, oat bran, ¼ cup sugar, baking powder, baking soda and salt in large bowl. Cut in butter with pastry blender or two knives until mixture resembles coarse crumbs. Stir in cranberries.

3. Whisk milk and egg in small bowl until well blended. Reserve 2 tablespoons milk mixture. Stir sour cream into remaining milk mixture. Add to flour mixture; stir just until soft dough forms.

4. Turn out dough onto lightly floured surface; gently knead 10 to 12 times. Pat dough into 9×6-inch rectangle. Cut into six 3-inch squares with floured knife; cut diagonally into halves to form 12 triangles. Place 2 inches apart on ungreased baking sheet. Brush with reserved milk mixture; sprinkle with oats, if desired, and remaining 1 tablespoon sugar.

5. Bake 10 to 12 minutes or until golden brown. Remove to wire rack to cool 10 minutes. Serve warm.

CONFETTI SCONES

2 teaspoons olive oil

⅓ cup minced red bell pepper

⅓ cup minced green bell pepper

½ teaspoon dried thyme

1 cup all-purpose flour

¼ cup whole wheat flour

1½ teaspoons baking powder

½ teaspoon baking soda

½ teaspoon sugar

¼ teaspoon ground red pepper

⅛ teaspoon salt

⅓ cup milk

⅓ cup sour cream

¼ cup grated Parmesan cheese

2 tablespoons minced green onion

Makes 24 scones

1. Preheat oven to 400°F. Line baking sheets with parchment paper.

2. Heat oil in small skillet over medium heat. Add bell peppers and thyme; cook and stir 5 minutes or until tender.

3. Combine all-purpose flour, whole wheat flour, baking powder, baking soda, sugar, red pepper and salt in large bowl. Combine milk, sour cream, Parmesan, green onion and bell pepper mixture in medium bowl; mix well. Add to flour mixture; stir just until sticky dough forms. (Do not overmix.) Drop dough by rounded tablespoonfuls onto prepared baking sheets.

4. Place in oven; *immediately reduce oven temperature to 375°F.* Bake 13 to 15 minutes or until golden brown. Remove to wire racks to cool 5 minutes. Serve warm.

LEMON-CARDAMOM SCONES

1¼ cups all-purpose flour

¾ cup oat bran

2 tablespoons granulated sugar

2 teaspoons grated lemon peel, divided

2 teaspoons baking powder

¾ teaspoon ground cardamom

¼ teaspoon baking soda

¼ teaspoon salt

¼ cup (½ stick) cold butter, cut into small pieces

1 container (6 ounces) lemon yogurt

1 egg

3 tablespoons powdered sugar

2 teaspoons lemon juice

Makes 8 servings

1. Preheat oven to 400°F. Spray baking sheet with nonstick cooking spray or line with parchment paper.

2. Combine flour, oat bran, granulated sugar, 1½ teaspoons lemon peel, baking powder, cardamom, baking soda and salt in large bowl. Cut in butter with pastry blender or two knives until mixture resembles coarse crumbs.

3. Whisk yogurt and egg in small bowl until well blended. Add to flour mixture; stir just until moistened.

4. Turn out dough onto lightly floured surface; gently knead 10 to 12 times. Pat dough into 7½-inch circle; cut into eight wedges. Place 2 inches apart on prepared baking sheet.

5. Bake 11 to 13 minutes or until golden brown. Remove to wire rack to cool 10 minutes.

6. Whisk powdered sugar, lemon juice and remaining ½ teaspoon lemon peel in small bowl until smooth. Drizzle glaze over scones.

Lemon-Ginger Scones: Substitute ground ginger for ground cardamom.

BISCUITS

CORN AND SUNFLOWER SEED BISCUITS

2 cups all-purpose flour

4 teaspoons baking powder

1 tablespoon sugar

½ teaspoon salt

½ teaspoon dried thyme

⅓ cup cold butter, cut into small pieces

1 cup milk

1 cup corn*

½ cup salted roasted sunflower seeds, divided

*Use fresh or thawed frozen corn; do not use supersweet corn.

Makes 12 biscuits

1. Preheat oven to 400°F. Line baking sheet with parchment paper or spray with nonstick cooking spray.

2. Combine flour, baking powder, sugar, salt and thyme in large bowl. Cut in butter with pastry blender or two knives until mixture resembles coarse crumbs.

3. Add milk; stir gently to form soft sticky dough. Stir in corn and ⅓ cup sunflower seeds. Drop dough by ¼ cupfuls 2 inches apart onto prepared baking sheet. Sprinkle with remaining sunflower seeds.

4. Bake 18 to 20 minutes or until golden brown. Remove to wire rack to cool 5 minutes. Serve warm.

MUSTARD BEER BISCUITS

2 cups all-purpose flour

2 teaspoons baking powder

¾ teaspoon salt

¼ cup shortening

¼ cup (½ stick) cold butter, cut into small pieces

½ cup beer

1 tablespoon plus 1 teaspoon yellow mustard, divided

1 tablespoon milk

Makes about 12 biscuits

1. Preheat oven to 425°F. Spray baking sheet with nonstick cooking spray or line with parchment paper.

2. Combine flour, baking powder and salt in large bowl. Cut in shortening and butter with pastry blender or two knives until mixture resembles coarse crumbs. Combine beer and 1 tablespoon mustard in small bowl. Add to flour mixture; stir just until moistened.

3. Turn out dough onto floured surface; knead gently eight times. Pat to ½-inch thickness. Cut dough with 2-inch biscuit cutter. Reroll scraps and cut out additional biscuits. Place 2 inches apart on prepared baking sheet.

4. Whisk remaining 1 teaspoon mustard and milk in small bowl until blended. Brush over tops of biscuits.

5. Bake 13 minutes or until lightly browned. Remove to wire rack to cool 5 minutes. Serve warm.

HAM AND SWISS CHEESE BISCUITS ▶

2 cups all-purpose flour

2 teaspoons baking powder

½ teaspoon baking soda

½ cup (1 stick) cold butter, cut into small pieces

⅔ cup buttermilk

½ cup (2 ounces) shredded Swiss cheese

2 ounces ham, minced

Makes about 18 biscuits

1. Preheat oven to 450°F. Spray baking sheets with nonstick cooking spray.

2. Combine flour, baking powder and baking soda in medium bowl. Cut in butter with pastry blender or two knives until mixture resembles coarse crumbs. Add buttermilk; stir to form soft sticky dough. Stir in cheese and ham.

3. Turn out dough onto lightly floured surface; knead gently. Roll to ½-inch thickness. Cut dough with 2-inch biscuit cutter. Place 2 inches apart on prepared baking sheet.

4. Bake 10 minutes or until golden brown. Remove to wire rack to cool 5 minutes. Serve warm.

SWEET POTATO BISCUITS

2½ cups all-purpose flour

¼ cup packed brown sugar

1 tablespoon baking powder

¾ teaspoon salt

¾ teaspoon ground cinnamon

¼ teaspoon ground ginger

¼ teaspoon ground allspice

½ cup shortening

½ cup chopped pecans

¾ cup mashed canned sweet potatoes

½ cup milk

Makes about 12 biscuits

1. Preheat oven to 450°F.

2. Combine flour, brown sugar, baking powder, salt, cinnamon, ginger and allspice in medium bowl. Cut in shortening with pastry blender or two knives until mixture resembles coarse crumbs. Stir in pecans.

3. Beat sweet potatoes and milk in small bowl until smooth. Add to flour mixture; stir to form soft dough.

4. Turn out dough onto lightly floured surface; knead gently. Roll to ½-inch thickness. Cut dough with 2½-inch biscuit cutter. Place 2 inches apart on ungreased baking sheet.

5. Bake 12 to 14 minutes or until golden brown. Remove to wire rack to cool 5 minutes. Serve warm.

WHEATY CRANBERRY BUTTERMILK BISCUITS

1 **cup all-purpose flour**

1 **cup whole wheat flour**

3 **tablespoons sugar**

2½ **teaspoons baking powder**

½ **teaspoon salt**

½ **teaspoon baking soda**

½ **cup (1 stick) cold butter, cut into small pieces**

¾ **cup buttermilk**

½ **cup dried cranberries**

⅓ **cup all-bran cereal**

Makes 8 biscuits

1. Preheat oven to 425°F. Spray large baking sheet with nonstick cooking spray or line with parchment paper.

2. Combine all-purpose flour, whole wheat flour, sugar, baking powder, salt and baking soda in large bowl. Cut in butter with pastry blender or two knives until mixture resembles coarse crumbs.

3. Add buttermilk; stir to form soft sticky dough. Stir in cranberries and cereal.

4. Turn dough out onto lightly floured surface. Pat or roll to ¾-inch thickness. Cut dough with 2½-inch biscuit cutter. Place 2 inches apart on prepared baking sheet.

5. Bake 15 minutes or until golden brown. Remove to wire rack to cool 5 minutes. Serve wam.

SWEET CHERRY BISCUITS

2 cups all-purpose flour

2 tablespoons sugar

4 teaspoons baking powder

½ teaspoon salt

½ teaspoon dried rosemary

½ cup (1 stick) cold butter, cut into small pieces

¾ cup milk

½ cup dried sweetened cherries, chopped

Makes about 10 biscuits

1. Preheat oven to 425°F.

2. Combine flour, sugar, baking powder, salt and rosemary in large bowl. Cut in butter with pastry blender or two knives until mixture resembles coarse crumbs. Add milk; stir to form sticky dough. Stir in cherries.

3. Turn out dough onto floured surface. Pat or roll to 1-inch thickness. Cut dough with 3-inch biscuit cutter. Place 1 inch apart on ungreased baking sheet.

4. Bake 15 minutes or until golden brown. Remove to wire rack to cool 5 minutes. Serve warm.

YOGURT CHIVE BISCUITS

2 cups all-purpose flour

1 tablespoon sugar

2 teaspoons baking powder

½ teaspoon baking soda

½ teaspoon salt

¼ teaspoon dried oregano

¼ cup (½ stick) cold butter, cut into small pieces

⅔ cup plain Greek yogurt

½ cup milk

¼ cup sour cream

½ cup finely chopped fresh chives

Makes 12 biscuits

1. Preheat oven to 400°F. Line baking sheet with parchment paper or spray with nonstick cooking spray.

2. Combine flour, sugar, baking powder, baking soda, salt and oregano in large bowl. Cut in butter with pastry blender or two knives until coarse crumbs form.

3. Add yogurt, milk and sour cream; stir gently to form soft sticky dough. Stir in chives. Drop dough by ¼ cupfuls 2 inches apart onto prepared baking sheet.

4. Bake 15 to 16 minutes or until light golden brown. Remove to wire rack to cool 5 minutes. Serve warm.

Serving Suggestion: Split biscuits and top with a fried egg for a delicious breakfast or brunch.

CLASSIC BUTTERMILK BISCUITS

  2 **cups all-purpose flour**
  1 **tablespoon baking powder**
  2 **teaspoons sugar**
  ½ **teaspoon salt**
  ½ **teaspoon baking soda**
  ⅓ **cup shortening**
  ⅔ **cup buttermilk***

*Or substitute soured fresh milk. To sour milk, combine 2½ teaspoons lemon juice plus enough milk to equal ⅔ cup. Stir; let stand 5 minutes before using.

Makes about 9 biscuits

1. Preheat oven to 450°F.

2. Combine flour, baking powder, sugar, salt and baking soda in medium bowl. Cut in shortening with pastry blender or two knives until mixture resembles coarse crumbs. Make well in center of flour mixture. Add buttermilk; stir to form soft dough that clings together and forms a ball.

3. Turn out dough onto well-floured surface; knead gently 10 to 12 times. Roll or pat to ½-inch thickness. Cut dough with floured 2½-inch biscuit cutter. Place 2 inches apart on ungreased baking sheet.

4. Bake 8 to 10 minutes or until golden brown. Remove to wire rack to cool 5 minutes. Serve warm.

Drop Biscuits: Prepare Classic Buttermilk Biscuits as directed in step 2, increasing buttermilk to 1 cup. Stir batter with wooden spoon about 15 strokes. *Do not knead.* Drop dough by heaping tablespoonfuls 1 inch apart onto greased baking sheets. Bake as directed in step 4. Makes about 18 biscuits.

Bacon and Onion Biscuits: Prepare Classic Buttermilk Biscuits as directed in step 2, adding 4 slices crumbled crisp-cooked bacon and ⅓ cup chopped green onions to flour-shortening mixture before adding buttermilk. Continue as directed in steps 3 and 4. Makes about 9 biscuits.

GREEN ONION CREAM CHEESE BREAKFAST BISCUITS

2 cups all-purpose flour

1 tablespoon baking powder

1 tablespoon sugar

¾ teaspoon salt

3 ounces cold cream cheese, cut into small pieces

¼ cup shortening

½ cup finely chopped green onions

⅔ cup milk

Makes 8 biscuits

1. Preheat oven to 450°F.

2. Combine flour, baking powder, sugar and salt in medium bowl. Cut in cream cheese and shortening with pastry blender or two knives until mixture resembles coarse crumbs. Stir in green onions.

3. Make well in center of flour mixture. Add milk; stir to form soft dough that clings together and forms a ball.

4. Turn out dough onto well-floured surface; knead gently 10 to 12 times. Pat or roll to ½-inch thickness. Cut dough with floured 3-inch biscuit cutter. Place 2 inches apart on ungreased baking sheet.

5. Bake 10 to 12 minutes or until golden brown. Remove to wire rack to cool 5 minutes. Serve warm.

OATMEAL DROP BISCUITS ▶

1½ cups all-purpose flour

½ cup quick oats

1 tablespoon baking powder

2 teaspoons sugar

½ teaspoon salt

½ teaspoon grated orange peel

6 tablespoons (¾ stick) cold butter, cut into small pieces

¾ cup milk

Makes about 16 biscuits

1. Preheat oven to 450°F.

2. Combine flour, oats, baking powder, sugar, salt and orange peel in large bowl. Cut in butter with pastry blender or two knives until mixture resembles coarse crumbs.

3. Gently stir in ¼ cup milk. Stir in remaining milk, 1 tablespoon at a time, to form soft sticky dough. Drop dough by rounded tablespoonfuls 2 inches apart onto ungreased baking sheets.

4. Bake 10 to 12 minutes until golden brown. Remove to wire rack to cool 5 minutes. Serve warm.

PARMESAN PEPPERCORN BISCUITS

2 cups all-purpose flour

⅓ cup finely grated Parmesan cheese

1 tablespoon baking powder

1 teaspoon coarsely ground black pepper

½ teaspoon salt

6 tablespoons (¾ stick) cold butter, cut into small pieces

1 cup buttermilk

Makes 12 biscuits

1. Preheat oven to 425°F. Line baking sheet with parchment paper.

2. Combine flour, Parmesan, baking powder, pepper and salt in large bowl. Cut in butter with pastry blender or two knives until mixture resembles coarse crumbs.

3. Add buttermilk; stir just until moistened. Drop dough by ¼ cupfuls 2 inches apart onto prepared baking sheet.

4. Bake 12 minutes or until golden brown. Remove to wire rack to cool 5 minutes. Serve warm.

Gluten-Free
YEAST BREADS

ROSEMARY BREAD

2½ cups Gluten-Free Flour Blend for Breads (page 217), plus additional for pan

1 tablespoon active dry yeast (about 1½ packages)

1 tablespoon chopped fresh rosemary leaves

1½ teaspoons xanthan gum

1 teaspoon unflavored gelatin

½ teaspoon salt

2 eggs

¼ cup extra virgin olive oil

¾ cup warm whole milk (110° to 120°F)

Makes 1 loaf

1. Bring all ingredients to room temperature before preparing recipe. Spray 8×4-inch loaf pan with nonstick cooking spray; dust with flour blend.

2. Whisk 2½ cups flour blend, yeast, rosemary, xanthan gum, gelatin and salt in large bowl of stand mixer. Whisk eggs and oil in small bowl until well blended.

3. Add egg mixture to flour mixture; beat at low speed with paddle attachment until combined. Beat at high speed 3 to 4 minutes. (Batter should be smooth and stretchy.)

4. Spoon batter into prepared pan; level top with dampened fingers or oiled spoon. Cover loosely and let rise in warm place about 45 minutes or until batter comes within 1 inch of top of pan. Preheat oven to 400°F.

5. Bake 10 minutes. *Reduce oven temperature to 350°F.* Cover bread loosely with foil; bake 35 to 45 minutes or until bread sounds hollow when tapped and internal temperature is 190°F. Remove to wire rack to cool completely.

Tip: This bread will hold up to 2 days, well wrapped in the refrigerator. Freeze for longer storage.

GF SANDWICH BREAD

3 cups Gluten-Free Flour Blend
  for Breads (page 217),
  plus additional for pan

2 packages (¼ ounce each)
  active dry yeast

2 teaspoons xanthan gum

1 teaspoon salt

1 cup warm water, plus
  additional as needed

2 eggs

¼ cup vegetable oil

1 tablespoon honey

1 teaspoon cider vinegar

Makes 1 loaf

1. Line 9×5-inch loaf pan with foil, dull side out. (Do not use glass loaf pan.) Extend sides of foil 3 inches up from top of pan. Spray with nonstick cooking spray; dust with flour blend.

2. Whisk 3 cups flour blend, yeast, xanthan gum and salt in large bowl of stand mixer. Whisk 1 cup warm water, eggs, oil, honey and vinegar in medium bowl until well blended.

3. Add oil mixture to flour mixture; beat at low speed with paddle attachment until batter is smooth, shiny and thick. Add additional water, 1 tablespoon at a time, if necessary. Beat at medium-high speed 5 minutes, scraping side of bowl occasionally.

4. Spoon batter into prepared pan. Cover with lightly oiled plastic wrap; let rise in warm place 30 minutes or until batter reaches top of pan. Preheat oven to 375°F.

5. Bake 30 to 35 minutes or until bread sounds hollow when tapped and internal temperature is 200°F. Remove to wire rack to cool completely.

GLUTEN-FREE FLOUR BLEND FOR BREADS

- **1 cup brown rice flour**
- **1 cup sorghum flour**
- **1 cup tapioca flour**
- **1 cup cornstarch**
- **¾ cup millet flour***
- **⅓ cup instant mashed potato flakes**

*If millet flour is not available, substitute chickpea flour.

Makes about 5 cups

Combine all ingredients in large bowl. Whisk to make sure ingredients are evenly distributed. Recipe can be doubled or tripled. Store in airtight container in refrigerator.

OLIVE AND HERB FOCACCIA

3 cups Gluten-Free Flour Blend for Breads (page 217)

2 packages (¼ ounce each) active dry yeast

2 teaspoons xanthan gum

1 teaspoon salt

1¼ cups warm water (110°F), divided

3 egg whites

¼ cup extra virgin olive oil

1 tablespoon honey

1 teaspoon cider vinegar

Toppings

1 cup chopped pitted kalamata olives

3 tablespoons chopped fresh rosemary leaves

2 tablespoons chopped fresh thyme

3 cloves garlic, minced

¼ cup extra virgin olive oil

Salt and black pepper

¼ cup grated Romano cheese

Makes 8 to 10 servings

1. Whisk flour blend, yeast, xanthan gum and 1 teaspoon salt in large bowl of stand mixer. Whisk 1 cup warm water, egg whites, ¼ cup oil, honey and vinegar in medium bowl until well blended.

2. Add oil mixture to flour mixture; beat at low speed with paddle attachment until batter is smooth, shiny and thick. Add additional water, 1 tablespoon at a time, if necessary. Beat at medium-high speed 5 minutes, scraping side of bowl occasionally.

3. Preheat oven to 450°F. Line two pizza pans or baking sheets with parchment paper or foil. Place dough in center of prepared pans. Spread dough into 8-inch rounds, about ½ inch thick, with dampened hands. Cover and let rest 20 minutes.

4. Dimple tops of dough with fingertips or back of wooden spoon. Sprinkle evenly with olives, rosemary, thyme and garlic. Drizzle with ¼ cup oil; sprinkle with salt and pepper.

5. Bake 15 minutes or until lightly browned. Immediately sprinkle with Romano. Remove to wire rack to cool slightly. Serve warm.

GF CINNAMON RAISIN BREAD

3 cups Gluten-Free Flour Blend for Breads (page 217), plus additional for pan

⅓ cup sugar

1 tablespoon ground cinnamon

2 packages (¼ ounce each) active dry yeast

2 teaspoons xanthan gum

1 teaspoon salt

1¼ cups plus 2 tablespoons warm milk, divided

2 eggs

¼ cup vegetable oil

1 tablespoon honey or maple syrup

1 teaspoon cider vinegar

¾ cup raisins

1 tablespoon gluten-free oats (optional)

Makes 1 loaf

1. Line 9×5-inch loaf pan with foil, dull side out. (Do not use glass loaf pan.) Extend sides of foil 3 inches up from top of pan. Spray with nonstick cooking spray; dust with flour blend.

2. Combine sugar and cinnamon in small bowl; mix well. Set aside.

3. Whisk 3 cups flour blend, yeast, xanthan gum and salt in large bowl of stand mixer. Whisk 1¼ cups warm milk, eggs, oil, honey and vinegar in medium bowl until well blended. Add to flour mixture; beat at low speed with paddle attachment until batter is smooth, shiny and thick. Beat at medium-high speed 5 minutes, scraping side of bowl occasionally. Stir in raisins.

4. Preheat oven to 375°F. Place large sheet of parchment paper on work surface; sprinkle with flour blend. Scoop batter onto center of paper. Using dampened hands or oiled spatula, spread batter into 18×9-inch rectangle. Brush with remaining 2 tablespoons milk. Sprinkle with all but 1 tablespoon cinnamon-sugar, leaving 1-inch border.

5. Using parchment paper, roll up dough jelly-roll style, starting with short end. Push ends in to fit length of pan; trim excess paper. Using parchment paper, lift roll and place in prepared pan. (Leave parchment paper in pan.) Sprinkle with remaining 1 tablespoon cinnamon-sugar and oats, if desired.

6. Bake 35 to 45 minutes or until bread sounds hollow when tapped and internal temperature is 200°F. Remove bread from pan; remove parchment paper and foil. Cool completely on wire rack.

ASIAGO GARLIC ROLLS

1 **package (¼ ounce) active dry yeast**

1 **teaspoon sugar**

1 **cup warm water (110°F)**

1½ **cups Gluten-Free Flour Blend for Breads (page 217)**

½ **cup cornstarch**

¼ **cup almond flour**

1¼ **teaspoons xanthan gum**

1 **teaspoon unflavored gelatin or powdered pectin**

½ **teaspoon salt**

3 **eggs**

¼ **cup extra virgin olive oil**

½ **teaspoon cider vinegar**

½ **cup plus 2 tablespoons grated Asiago cheese, divided**

6 **cloves roasted garlic***

1 **tablespoon chopped fresh rosemary leaves**

To roast garlic, preheat oven to 375°F. Remove outer layers of papery skin and cut off top of garlic head. Place cut side up on piece of heavy-duty foil. Drizzle with 2 teaspoons olive oil; wrap tightly in foil. Bake 25 to 30 minutes or until cloves feel soft when pressed. Cool slightly before squeezing out garlic pulp.

Makes 12 rolls

1. Spray 12 standard (2½-inch) muffin cups with nonstick cooking spray. DIssolve yeast and sugar in warm water in small bowl; let stand 10 minutes or until bubbly.

2. Whisk flour blend, cornstarch, almond flour, xanthan gum, gelatin and salt in large bowl of stand mixer. Whisk eggs, oil and vinegar in medium bowl until well blended.

3. Add yeast mixture and egg mixture to flour mixture; beat at low speed with paddle attachment until blended. Add ½ cup Asiago, garlic and rosemary; beat at high speed 3 minutes or until smooth.

4. Spoon batter evenly into prepared muffin cups, Cover with plastic wrap sprayed with nonstick cooking spray; let rise in warm place 30 minutes. Preheat oven to 375°F.

5. Bake 15 minutes. Sprinkle rolls with remaining 2 tablespoons Asiago; bake 5 to 10 minutes or until lightly browned. Remove to wire rack to cool completely.

CHILI CHEESE BREAD

1½ **cups Gluten-Free Flour Blend for Breads (page 217)**

1 **cup (4 ounces) shredded Cheddar cheese**

1 **tablespoon sugar**

1 **tablespoon chili powder**

1 **package (¼ ounce) active dry yeast**

1½ **teaspoons xanthan gum**

1 **teaspoon unflavored gelatin**

½ **teaspoon salt**

¾ **cup water**

2 **eggs**

3 **tablespoons olive oil**

Makes 1 loaf

1. Spray 8×4-inch loaf pan with nonstick cooking spray.

2. Whisk flour blend, cheese, sugar, chili powder, yeast, xanthan gum, gelatin and salt in medium bowl. Beat water, eggs and oil in large bowl with electric mixer at medium speed until well blended.

3. Gradually add flour mixture to egg mixture; beat at low speed with paddle attachment 10 minutes. Batter will be sticky and stretchy. Spoon batter into prepared pan.

4. Cover and let rise in warm place about 1 hour or until dough almost reaches top of pan. Preheat oven to 350°F.

5. Bake 40 to 50 minutes or until bread sounds hollow when tapped and internal temperature is 190°F. (Check after 20 minutes and cover with foil if bread is browning too quickly.) Cool in pan on wire rack 10 minutes; remove to wire rack to cool completely.

GLUTEN-FREE PIZZA

1¾ cups Gluten-Free Flour Blend for Breads (page 217), plus additional for work surface

1½ cups white rice flour

2 teaspoons sugar

1 package (¼ ounce) active dry yeast

1½ teaspoons salt

1½ teaspoons Italian seasoning

1 teaspoon baking powder

½ teaspoon xanthan gum

1¼ cups warm water (110°F)

2 tablespoons olive oil

Toppings: gluten-free pizza sauce, fresh mozzarella cheese, sliced tomatoes, fresh basil, grated Parmesan cheese

Makes 4 to 6 servings

1. Whisk flour blend, 1½ cups rice flour, sugar, yeast, salt, Italian seasoning, baking powder and xanthan gum in large bowl of stand mixer. Gradually add warm water; beat at low speed with paddle attachment until soft dough forms. Add oil; beat 2 minutes.

2. Turn out dough onto floured surface; knead 2 minutes or until dough forms a smooth ball.

3. Place dough in greased bowl; turn to grease top. Cover and let rise in warm place 30 minutes. (Dough will increase in size but not double.)

4. Preheat oven to 400°F. Line pizza pan or baking sheet with foil. Punch down dough; place in center of prepared pan. Spread dough as thin as possible (about ⅛ inch thick) using dampened hands.

5. Bake 5 to 7 minutes or until crust just begins to brown. (Crust may crack in spots.)

6. Top crust with desired toppings. Bake 10 to 15 minutes or until cheese is melted and crust is lightly browned.

MULTIGRAIN SANDWICH BREAD

1 cup brown rice flour, plus additional for pan

1¾ cups warm water (110°F)

2 tablespoons honey

1 tablespoon active dry yeast (about 1½ packages)

¾ cup white rice flour

⅔ cup dry milk powder

½ cup gluten-free oat flour

⅓ cup cornstarch

⅓ cup potato starch

¼ cup teff flour

2 teaspoons xanthan gum

2 teaspoons egg white powder

1½ teaspoons salt

1 teaspoon unflavored gelatin

2 eggs

¼ cup canola oil

Makes 1 loaf

1. Preheat oven to 350°F. Spray 9×5-inch loaf pan with nonstick cooking spray; dust with brown rice flour.

2. Combine warm water and honey in medium bowl. Stir in yeast; let stand 5 minutes or until bubbly.

3. Whisk 1 cup brown rice flour, white rice flour, milk powder, oat flour, cornstarch, potato starch, teff flour, xanthan gum, egg white powder, salt and gelatin in large bowl of stand mixer. Whisk eggs and oil in small bowl until well blended.

4. Gradually add yeast mixture and egg mixture to flour mixture; beat at low speed with paddle attachment until blended. Beat at high speed 5 minutes or until smooth. Pour batter into prepared pan.

5. Bake 1 hour or until internal temperature reaches 200°F. Remove to wire rack to cool completely.

GF BREADSTICKS

3½ cups Gluten-Free Flour Blend
    for Breads (page 217)
  1 package (¼ ounce) active
    dry yeast
  3 teaspoons salt, divided
1½ teaspoons xanthan gum
  1 teaspoon unflavored gelatin
1⅓ cups warm water
  ¼ cup olive oil, divided
  1 tablespoon honey
  2 to 4 cloves garlic, minced

Makes 15 to 20 breadsticks

1. Combine flour blend, yeast, 2 teaspoons salt, xanthan gum and gelatin in food processor; process until blended. With motor running, add warm water, 2 tablespoons oil and honey; process 30 seconds or until well blended. (Dough will be sticky.)

2. Shape dough into a ball with dampened hands. Place dough in greased bowl; turn to grease top. Cover and let rise in warm place 45 minutes.

3. Punch down dough; let rest 15 minutes. Preheat oven to 450°F. Line baking sheets with parchment paper.

4. Roll 1½-inch portions of dough into 8-inch-long ropes on clean work surface. Place on prepared baking sheets.

5. Bake 10 minutes. Meanwhile, combine remaining 2 tablespoons oil and garlic in small bowl; mix well. Brush rolls with garlic mixture; bake 10 minutes or until browned. Remove to wire racks to cool slightly. Serve warm.

Variation: For a sesame seed or poppy seed topping, brush breadsticks lightly with water and sprinkle evenly with seeds before baking.

Tip: Be sure to rotate pans once during baking so the breadsticks brown evenly.

Gluten-Free
BREAD BASKET

LEMON POPPY SEED MUFFINS

2 cups Gluten-Free All-Purpose Flour Blend (page 235)*

1¼ cups granulated sugar

¼ cup poppy seeds

3 tablespoons grated lemon peel, divided

1 tablespoon baking powder

¾ teaspoon xanthan gum

½ teaspoon baking soda

½ teaspoon ground cardamom

¼ teaspoon salt

2 eggs

½ cup (1 stick) butter, melted

½ cup milk

½ cup plus 2 tablespoons lemon juice, divided

1 cup powdered sugar

*Or use any all-purpose gluten-free flour blend that does not contain xanthan gum.

Makes 18 muffins

1. Preheat oven to 400°F. Line 18 standard (2½-inch) muffin cups with paper baking cups or spray with nonstick cooking spray.

2. Combine flour blend, granulated sugar, poppy seeds, 2 tablespoons lemon peel, baking powder, xanthan gum, baking soda, cardamom and salt in large bowl.

3. Whisk eggs in medium bowl. Add butter, milk and ½ cup lemon juice; whisk until well blended. Add to flour mixture; stir just until moistened. Spoon batter evenly into prepared muffin cups.

4. Bake 15 to 20 minutes or until toothpick inserted into centers comes out clean. Cool in pans on wire racks 10 minutes.

5. Combine powdered sugar and 2 teaspoons lemon peel in small bowl; stir in enough remaining lemon juice to make pourable glaze. Place muffins on sheet of foil or waxed paper. Spoon glaze over muffins; sprinkle with remaining 1 teaspoon lemon peel. Serve warm or cool completely.

ZUCCHINI BREAD

2½ cups Gluten-Free All-Purpose Flour Blend (page 235)*

⅔ cup packed brown sugar

½ cup teff flour**

⅓ cup granulated sugar

1 tablespoon baking powder

2 teaspoons ground cinnamon

1 teaspoon baking soda

1 teaspoon salt

¾ teaspoon xanthan gum

¼ teaspoon ground allspice

¼ teaspoon ground nutmeg

¼ teaspoon ground cardamom

1¼ cups whole milk

2 eggs

¼ cup canola oil

1 teaspoon vanilla

1½ cups grated zucchini, squeezed dry

*Or use any all-purpose gluten-free flour blend that does not contain xanthan gum.

Makes 1 loaf

1. Preheat oven to 350°F. Spray 9×5-inch loaf pan with nonstick cooking spray.

2. Combine flour blend, brown sugar, teff flour, granulated sugar, baking powder, cinnamon, baking soda, salt, xanthan gum, allspice, nutmeg and cardamom in large bowl. Whisk milk, eggs, oil and vanilla in medium bowl until well blended.

3. Add milk mixture to flour mixture; stir just until moistened. Stir in zucchini. Pour batter into prepared pan.

4. Bake 1 hour or until toothpick inserted into center comes out almost clean. Cool in pan on wire rack 5 minutes; remove to wire rack to cool completely.

GLUTEN-FREE ALL-PURPOSE FLOUR BLEND

- **1 cup white rice flour**
- **1 cup sorghum flour**
- **1 cup tapioca flour**
- **1 cup cornstarch**
- **1 cup almond flour or coconut flour**

Combine all ingredients in large bowl. Whisk to make sure flours are evenly distributed. Recipe can be doubled or tripled. Store in airtight container in refrigerator.

Makes about 5 cups

CINNAMON SCONES

2 cups Gluten-Free All-
Purpose Flour Blend
(page 235),* plus
additional for work surface

¼ cup sugar

2½ teaspoons baking powder

¾ teaspoon salt

¾ teaspoon xanthan gum

½ teaspoon baking soda

½ cup (1 stick) cold butter,
cut into small pieces

⅓ cup cinnamon chips

¾ cup whole milk

½ cup plain low-fat yogurt

2 tablespoons cinnamon-sugar

*Or use any all-purpose gluten-free flour
blend that does not contain xanthan gum.*

Makes 12 scones

1. Preheat oven to 425°F. Line baking sheet with parchment paper.

2. Combine 2 cups flour blend, sugar, baking powder, salt, xanthan gum and baking soda in large bowl. Cut in butter with pastry blender or two knives until coarse crumbs form. Stir in cinnamon chips.

3. Whisk milk and yogurt in small bowl until well blended. Gradually add to flour mixture; stir just until dough forms. (You may not need all of milk mixture.)

4. Turn out dough onto floured surface; knead five or six times until dough holds together.

5. Divide dough into two pieces. Pat each piece into 5-inch circle about ½ inch thick. Cut each circle into six wedges with floured knife. Place 2 inches apart on prepared baking sheet. Sprinkle with cinnamon-sugar.

6. Bake 10 to 14 minutes or until lightly browned. Remove to wire rack to cool completely.

PIÑA COLADA MUFFINS

2 cups Gluten-Free All-Purpose Flour Blend (page 235)*

¾ cup sugar

½ cup flaked coconut

1 tablespoon baking powder

1 teaspoon xanthan gum

½ teaspoon baking soda

½ teaspoon salt

2 eggs

1 cup sour cream

1 can (8 ounces) crushed pineapple in juice, undrained

¼ cup (½ stick) butter, melted

⅛ teaspoon coconut extract

Additional flaked coconut (optional)

*Or use any all-purpose gluten-free flour blend that does not contain xanthan gum.

Makes 18 muffins

1. Preheat oven to 400°F. Line 18 standard (2½-inch) muffin cups with paper baking cups or spray with nonstick cooking spray.

2. Combine flour blend, sugar, coconut, baking powder, xanthan gum, baking soda and salt in large bowl.

3. Whisk eggs in medium bowl. Add sour cream, pineapple with juice, butter and coconut extract; whisk until well blended. Add to flour mixture; stir just until moistened. Spoon batter evenly into prepared muffin cups.

4. Bake 15 to 20 minutes or until toothpick inserted into centers comes out clean. If desired, sprinkle tops of muffins with additional coconut after first 10 minutes of baking time. Cool in pans on wire racks 2 minutes; remove to wire racks to cool completely.

ORANGE-LEMON CITRUS BREAD

1¾ cups Gluten-Free All-Purpose Flour Blend (recipe follows),* plus additional for pan

¾ cup sugar

1 tablespoon plus ½ teaspoon grated lemon peel, divided

2 teaspoons baking powder

1 teaspoon xanthan gum

¼ teaspoon salt

1 cup milk

½ cup vegetable oil

1 egg

1 teaspoon vanilla

¼ cup orange marmalade

Or use any all-purpose gluten-free flour blend that does not contain xanthan gum.

Makes 1 loaf

1. Preheat oven to 350°F. Spray 9×5-inch loaf pan with nonstick cooking spray; dust with flour blend.

2. Combine 1¾ cups flour blend, sugar, 1 tablespoon lemon peel, baking powder, xanthan gum and salt in large bowl. Whisk milk, oil, egg and vanilla in small bowl until well blended.

3. Add milk mixture to flour mixture; stir just until blended. (Batter will be thin.) Pour batter into prepared pan.

4. Bake 45 minutes or until toothpick inserted into center comes out clean. Cool in pan on wire rack 5 minutes.

5. Meanwhile, combine marmalade and remaining ½ teaspoon lemon peel in small microwavable bowl. Microwave on HIGH 15 seconds or until slightly melted.

6. Remove bread to wire rack; spread marmalade mixture evenly over top of loaf. Cool completely on wire rack.

GLUTEN-FREE PUMPKIN MUFFINS

2¼ cups Gluten-Free All-
    Purpose Flour Blend
    (page 235)*

½ teaspoon salt

½ teaspoon ground ginger

½ teaspoon ground nutmeg

½ teaspoon xanthan gum

¼ teaspoon baking soda

1 cup packed dark brown
    sugar

1 cup canned solid-pack
    pumpkin

½ cup (1 stick) butter, melted

2 eggs

¼ cup buttermilk

3 tablespoons molasses

1 teaspoon vanilla

*Or use any all-purpose gluten-free flour
blend that does not contain xanthan gum.*

Makes 12 muffins

1. Preheat oven to 400°F. Spray 12 standard (2½-inch) muffin cups with nonstick cooking spray.

2. Combine flour blend, salt, ginger, nutmeg, xanthan gum and baking soda in medium bowl. Whisk brown sugar, pumpkin, butter, eggs, buttermilk, molasses and vanilla in large bowl until well blended.

3. Add flour mixture to pumpkin mixture in two parts, stirring until well blended after each addition. Spoon batter evenly into prepared muffin cups.**

4. Bake 18 to 22 minutes or until toothpick inserted into centers comes out clean. Cool in pan 5 minutes; remove to wire rack. Serve warm or cool completely.

**For best results, scoop batter into each muffin cup in a single scoop, filling to the top; do not add additional batter.

CHOCOLATE CHIP ELVIS BREAD

2½ cups Gluten-Free All-Purpose Flour Blend (page 235)*

½ cup granulated sugar

½ cup packed brown sugar

1 tablespoon baking powder

1 teaspoon xanthan gum

¾ teaspoon salt

1 cup mashed ripe bananas (about 2 large)

1 cup rice milk

¾ cup peanut butter

¼ cup vegetable oil

1 egg

1 teaspoon vanilla

1 cup semisweet chocolate chips

Or use any all-purpose gluten-free flour blend that does not contain xanthan gum.

Makes 4 mini loaves

1. Preheat oven to 350°F. Spray 4 mini (5×3-inch) or 2 (8×4-inch) loaf pans with nonstick cooking spray.

2. Combine flour blend, granulated sugar, brown sugar, baking powder, xanthan gum and salt in large bowl. Beat bananas, milk, peanut butter, oil, egg and vanilla in medium bowl until well blended.

3. Add banana mixture and chocolate chips to flour mixture; stir just until moistened. Pour batter into prepared pans.

4. Bake 40 minutes or until toothpick inserted into centers comes out clean (45 to 50 minutes for 8×4-inch pans). Cool in pans on wire racks 10 minutes; remove to wire racks to cool completely.

APPLESAUCE MUFFINS

2 cups Gluten-Free All-Purpose Flour Blend (page 235)*

½ cup plus 3 tablespoons granulated sugar, divided

½ cup plus 3 tablespoons packed brown sugar, divided

4 teaspoons ground cinnamon, divided

2 teaspoons baking powder

1 teaspoon baking soda

1 teaspoon xanthan gum

½ cup chunky applesauce

½ cup vegetable oil

½ cup apple cider

2 eggs, beaten

3 tablespoons butter, melted

Powdered sugar (optional)

Or use any all-purpose gluten-free flour blend that does not contain xanthan gum.

Makes 16 muffins

1. Preheat oven to 350°F. Line 16 standard (2½-inch) muffin cups with paper baking cups.

2. Combine flour blend, ½ cup granulated sugar, ½ cup brown sugar, 3 teaspoons cinnamon, baking powder, baking soda and xanthan gum in large bowl. Add applesauce, oil, apple cider and eggs; stir until well blended. Spoon batter evenly into prepared muffin cups.

3. Combine remaining 3 tablespoons granulated sugar, 3 tablespoons brown sugar, 1 teaspoon cinnamon and butter in small bowl; stir with fork until small clumps form. Sprinkle evenly over muffins.

4. Bake 25 to 30 minutes. Cool in pans on wire racks 5 minutes; remove to wire racks to cool completely. Sprinkle with powdered sugar, if desired.

APRICOT CRANBERRY SCONES

2 cups Gluten-Free All-Purpose Flour Blend (page 235),* plus additional for work surface

¼ cup sugar

2½ teaspoons baking powder

¾ teaspoon salt

¾ teaspoon xanthan gum

½ teaspoon baking soda

¼ cup chopped dried apricots

¼ cup dried cranberries

½ cup (1 stick) cold butter, cut into small pieces

¾ cup milk

½ cup plain yogurt

*Or use any all-purpose gluten-free flour blend that does not contain xanthan gum.

Makes about 15 scones

1. Preheat oven to 425°F. Line baking sheet with parchment paper.

2. Combine 2 cups flour blend, sugar, baking powder, salt, xanthan gum and baking soda in large bowl. Stir in apricots and cranberries. Cut in butter with pastry blender or two knives until coarse crumbs form.

3. Whisk milk and yogurt in small bowl until well blended. Gradually add to flour mixture; stir just until dough forms. (You may not need all of milk mixture.)

4. Turn out dough onto floured surface; knead five or six times until dough holds together. Pat into circle about ½ inch thick. Cut dough with floured 2-inch biscuit cutter. Place 2 inches apart on prepared baking sheet. Press together remaining dough; cut out additional scones.

5. Bake 10 to 14 minutes or until lightly browned. Remove to wire rack to cool completely.

BUTTERMILK DROP BISCUITS

2 cups Gluten-Free All-
  Purpose Flour Blend
  (page 235)*

2 teaspoons baking powder

1½ teaspoons xanthan gum

1 teaspoon sugar

½ teaspoon salt

¼ teaspoon baking soda

1 cup buttermilk

5 tablespoons butter,
  melted, divided

Or use any all-purpose gluten-free flour blend that does not contain xanthan gum.

Makes 9 biscuits

1. Preheat oven to 450°F. Line baking sheet with parchment paper or spray with nonstick cooking spray.

2. Combine flour blend, baking powder, xanthan gum, sugar, salt and baking soda in large bowl. Whisk buttermilk and 4 tablespoons butter in small bowl until well blended. Add to flour mixture; stir just until blended.

3. Using ¼ cup measuring cup sprayed with cooking spray, drop biscuits 2 inches apart onto prepared baking sheet.

4. Bake 12 minutes or until golden brown. Brush tops of biscuits with remaining 1 tablespoon butter. Cool on baking sheet 5 minutes. Serve warm.

METRIC CONVERSION CHART

VOLUME MEASUREMENTS (dry)

$^1/_8$ teaspoon = 0.5 mL
$^1/_4$ teaspoon = 1 mL
$^1/_2$ teaspoon = 2 mL
$^3/_4$ teaspoon = 4 mL
1 teaspoon = 5 mL
1 tablespoon = 15 mL
2 tablespoons = 30 mL
$^1/_4$ cup = 60 mL
$^1/_3$ cup = 75 mL
$^1/_2$ cup = 125 mL
$^2/_3$ cup = 150 mL
$^3/_4$ cup = 175 mL
1 cup = 250 mL
2 cups = 1 pint = 500 mL
3 cups = 750 mL
4 cups = 1 quart = 1 L

VOLUME MEASUREMENTS (fluid)

1 fluid ounce (2 tablespoons) = 30 mL
4 fluid ounces ($^1/_2$ cup) = 125 mL
8 fluid ounces (1 cup) = 250 mL
12 fluid ounces (1$^1/_2$ cups) = 375 mL
16 fluid ounces (2 cups) = 500 mL

WEIGHTS (mass)

$^1/_2$ ounce = 15 g
1 ounce = 30 g
3 ounces = 90 g
4 ounces = 120 g
8 ounces = 225 g
10 ounces = 285 g
12 ounces = 360 g
16 ounces = 1 pound = 450 g

DIMENSIONS

$^1/_{16}$ inch = 2 mm
$^1/_8$ inch = 3 mm
$^1/_4$ inch = 6 mm
$^1/_2$ inch = 1.5 cm
$^3/_4$ inch = 2 cm
1 inch = 2.5 cm

OVEN TEMPERATURES

250°F = 120°C
275°F = 140°C
300°F = 150°C
325°F = 160°C
350°F = 180°C
375°F = 190°C
400°F = 200°C
425°F = 220°C
450°F = 230°C

BAKING PAN SIZES

Utensil	Size in Inches/Quarts	Metric Volume	Size in Centimeters
Baking or Cake Pan (square or rectangular)	8×8×2	2 L	20×20×5
	9×9×2	2.5 L	23×23×5
	12×8×2	3 L	30×20×5
	13×9×2	3.5 L	33×23×5
Loaf Pan	8×4×3	1.5 L	20×10×7
	9×5×3	2 L	23×13×7
Round Layer Cake Pan	8×1½	1.2 L	20×4
	9×1½	1.5 L	23×4
Pie Plate	8×1¼	750 mL	20×3
	9×1¼	1 L	23×3
Baking Dish or Casserole	1 quart	1 L	—
	1½ quart	1.5 L	—
	2 quart	2 L	—